Jacob Gould Schurman

Agnosticism and Religion

Jacob Gould Schurman

Agnosticism and Religion

ISBN/EAN: 9783337132361

Printed in Europe, USA, Canada, Australia, Japan

Cover: Foto ©ninafisch / pixelio.de

More available books at **www.hansebooks.com**

·AGNOSTICISM AND RELIGION

BY

JACOB GOULD SCHURMAN

President of Cornell University

NEW YORK

CHARLES SCRIBNER'S SONS

1896

" *The dogmas of the quiet past are inadequate to the stormy present. The occasion is piled high with difficulty, and we must rise with the occasion. As our case is new, so we must think anew, and act anew. We must disenthrall ourselves, and then we shall save our [religion].*"

CONTENTS

———◦◦◦———

PART I

PART II

PART III

vii

PART I

HUXLEY AND SCIENTIFIC AGNOSTICISM

"Thou fool, that which thou sowest is not quickened, except it die."

HUXLEY AND SCIENTIFIC
AGNOSTICISM[1]

I DO not think I can, at the beginning
of this new academic year, better minister
to your spiritual needs than by inviting
you, in the solemn calm of this time and
place, to reflect for an hour with me upon
the vital doctrines of the distinguished
investigator and thinker who during the
summer has been snatched by death from
the ranks of science, of which for more than
a third of a century he has been a fruitful
cultivator, a doughty defender, and an illustrious ornament. It was on Saturday,
June 29th, that Professor Huxley passed
away, encountering the great mystery
which closes the continuous mystery of
life a few weeks after filling out the psalmist's measure of threescore years and ten.
His death is a severe, and but for his work

[1] An address delivered before the students of Cornell University, Sunday evening, November 3, 1895.

3

it would be an irreparable, loss to the republic of thought and science. And, in
voicing the sincere regret we all feel at
the removal of this brilliant and devoted
worker for the enlargement and defence
of human knowledge, I desire, while dis-
charging what you will perhaps permit me
to regard as a corporate trust, to express,
if it is not presumptuous, my personal appreciation of his abilities and attainments
and my respect for the integrity of his
character, the nobility of his aims, and
the apostolic zeal and earnestness with
which he devoted himself to the work of
his life. I embrace this opportunity the
more eagerly as I am constrained to dissent
from some of Huxley's views.

Thomas Henry Huxley was born on the
4th of May, 1825. His early education
was somewhat irregular. While still a
boy, he had a strong desire to be a mechanical engineer ; and, if his architectonic genius, clear intellect, and enthusiastic and
aggressive energy had been enlisted in the
engineering profession, it is impossible to
say what he might not have achieved ; but
I much doubt if the modern world, whose
civilization is nourished by heat, would

still be guilty of the stupid and wanton waste of nine tenths of the energy stored up in coal for the purpose of making the remaining tenth available. But it was not destined that Huxley should solve this still unsolved problem. At an early age he entered upon the study of medicine, and in the first M.B. examination at the University of London he took honors in anatomy and physiology. His taste for engineering did not leave him; the arena for its exercise was merely shifted from the inorganic macrocosm to the organic microcosm, — from nature to the living body. He cared little about medicine as the art of healing; the only subject in his professional course which really and deeply interested him was physiology, — and physiology conceived as "the mechanical engineering of living machines." With the genius of a Watt or Edison he set himself to work out the unity of plan in the structures of the innumerable throngs of diverse living beings and the modifications made in the same fundamental mechanism to serve diverse ends. Fortune favored his tastes and ambition. The captain of Her Majesty's ship *Rattlesnake*, which had been ordered to make a surveying voyage in the southern seas, wanted for assistant surgeon a man who knew something of science; and through the influence of Sir John Richardson, the distinguished naturalist and Arctic explorer, Huxley was given the appointment. For more than four years — from 1846 to 1850 — he studied in Nature's great biological laboratory, as Darwin and Hooker had done before him, spending most of his time on the coasts of Australia and New Guinea. The communications he sent home won him a reputation in the scientific world; and in 1851 he was elected a Fellow of the Royal Society. He now desired to obtain a professorship of either Physiology or Comparative Anatomy; but he was unsuccessful in all his applications. With his friend Tyndall, he turned his eyes to the New World; but the University of Toronto, in which at the same time they became candidates for the vacant chairs of Physics and Natural History, "would not look at either" of them. In 1854, however, Sir Henry De la Beche, the Director-General of the Geological Survey, offered Huxley the post of Palæontologist and Lecturer on Natural History which Forbes had just resigned in the Royal School of Mines in order to accept the chair of Natural History in Edinburgh University. Huxley was divided between his allegiance to physiology and his desire for the professorship. He frankly told Sir Henry that he did not care for fossils and that he would give up Natural History as soon as he could get a chair of Physiology. But, as General Grant said, on publishing his Memoirs after having determined never to write anything for publication: "There are but few important events in the affairs of men brought about by their own choice." Not only did Huxley become Lecturer on Natural History, but he held the office for thirty-one years; and of his scientific work a large part is palæontological. Indeed, he took the whole field of zoölogy for his province; and it is the verdict of Haeckel that he was the foremost zoölogist in England. This is not the place to describe his volumes or even to mention his celebrated memoirs. After the publication of the "Origin of Species," his investigations were largely guided by the Darwinian hypothesis, of which his results formed a striking and substantial verification. While his research embraced both vertebrate and invertebrate life, he gave special attention to the structure and functions of vertebrate animals and he won renown by his brilliant elucidations of the intricacies of their mechanism. His growing fame procured him membership and office in many learned institutions and scientific associations; and in 1883 he was crowned with the highest official distinction to which a British scientist can aspire, the presidency of the Royal Society, — of which for ten years he had been the secretary. In 1885 he resigned his professorship (at sixty, he used to say, every scientific man "should commit the happy despatch") and all his other official posts, and soon afterwards removed from London to Eastbourne. But, though he had well earned the ease and quiet of retirement, it is the last decade of his life which is notably marked by those divagations into politics, ethics, and especially theology, which made Huxley's name one of the best known in current literature. These incursions were often resisted, but such was the advantage of his controversial position and his skill in attack and defence that he was seldom worsted and never vanquished, though he had among his adversaries some of the subtlest disputants in the English-speaking world.

For Huxley was not merely a seeker of truth, he was her knight and sworn champion, her defender and her advocate. To carry the " platform " of science with the "intelligent electors " of the commonwealth was, I think, his dearest ambition. But he would have been as good a champion of any other "platform" which he had once accepted with that intense intellectual impulsiveness he inherited from his mother. Indeed, I suspect that the Genius which presides over the nativity of Englishmen may have intended him for leader of the opposition to Her Majesty's government in the House of Commons ; but the accident of a "medical brother-in-law" made him a biologist ; and so it happened that the combativeness, the genius for debate, the skill in attack and defence, the courage and audacity, and all the splendid fighting qualities with which Nature had endowed this ardent and iconoclastic radical were destined to find a field of activity in the advocacy of scientific knowledge and the defiance and denunciation of conventional Christianity. He says himself that he could not count even his scientific attainments and honors " as marks of success if I could not hope that I had somewhat helped that movement of opinion which has been called the New Reformation." He dearly loved a tilt with the ecclesiastical opponents of this progressive theology. And not even in the British Parliament was there a more formidable controversialist in England. Always courteous, he had at command the resources of ridicule and sarcasm ; warmly devoted to truth, he possessed an unerring sense for falsehood and error ; master of a lucid and trenchant style, a skilful dialectician, and a wonderful adept in the art of luminous explanation and popular exposition, he was at home in science, he had travelled the highways of modern philosophy and literature, and, as Burke said of Charles Townshend, he knew how to bring together, within a short time, all that was necessary to establish, to illustrate, and to decorate that side of the question he supported. Nor was this all.

The strong atmosphere of debate and contention was to Huxley like the air of the sea or mountain. His zest in the pursuit of knowledge was never quite so keen as when the game led across the enemy's preserve. He had, indeed, the idealist's faith, that truth would prevail, but he delighted to abound in militant works for the removal of obstacles that impeded her victorious march. Darwin passed his life in serene contemplation and studious investigation of nature, interrupted only by the thrill of fresh insight and the ecstasy of new discoveries. Huxley liked research too ; but he cared more for the general acceptance of the results achieved by scientists, and his chief delight was in compelling the public to assent to them, unless, as one might sometimes suspect, he derived still greater satisfaction from confuting pretentious critics and ruthlessly exposing their ignorance. It is this missionary spirit which distinguished Huxley from all the scientists of his generation. He was the great apostle of the modern gospel of science. And as he had the preacher's earnestness in proclaiming this evangel and the controversialist's determination to make it prevail, so he had the dogmatist's immovable confidence that his creed was the only orthodox doctrine, and that it was destined to overcome all rival dogmas as the rod of Moses swallowed up the rods of the lesser magicians. He was of the same breed as the theologians he assailed. It matters not that theirs was the faith once delivered to the saints and his the creed gradually elaborated by the scientists. In his temper and mental habit, in his attitude towards what he believed the truth, Huxley was as veritable a dogmatist as any of his theological antagonists, though they banned what he blessed and though he was neither of Paul or Peter, but heartily wished a plague on both their houses. A scientist by profession and achievement, but inwardly a theological iconoclast, it is not strange that, with his gifts and under the stimulus of favoring circumstances, Huxley should have become the most distinguished protagonist in the fierce scientific and theological controversies of his generation. He was still a young man — only thirty-four years of age — when the bitter warfare began in which for the remaining half of his life he drank delight of battle with his peers,

   " Far on the ringing plains of windy Troy."

The signal and the occasion of the impending storm was the appearance, in 1859, of Darwin's " Origin of Species." The tempest which this work aroused in the intellectual world was without a parallel since the time when Galileo, whom (sad irony of fate!) the youthful Milton found blind and a prisoner of the Inquisition, had revolutionized the thought of Christendom by inaugurating the Copernican astronomy. The Prospero who, in his innocency, had conjured up this storm was a modest, retiring, diffident country gentleman, peaceful as a Quaker, dreading controversy, avoiding society, and devoting his entire energy (whenever a fragile constitution permitted him to labor) to harmless observation of the ways of plants and animals and innocent reflection upon the mode of their development. This interpreter of nature was distinguished for his caution, his patience, and, above all, his fair-mindedness. Now, as a result of his study and meditation, he had come to the conclusion that biological species, which had hitherto passed for immutable creations, were the slowly consolidated growths of changing varieties. The ferment which Darwin thus cast into the mass of current beliefs was in its logical essence identical with Galileo's *e pur si muove*. The astronomer asserted that the earth moved; the biologist that species changed. But Darwin was more than a modern Heracleitus championing the heresy of flux in opposition to the orthodox tradition of fixity as the law of the organic world. Others, too, had dreamt of the natural transmutation of species as an alternative to the miracle of creation. Darwin endeavored to turn the dream into a demonstration. His is the peculiar glory of actually showing, by analogy of the selective breeding practised by horticulturists and agriculturists, how the variations in the species of plants and animals which are constantly turning up are, under the influence of what he called Natural Selection, preserved, and then transmitted with modifications to descendants, until by successive accumulations they are consolidated into species

entirely distinct from the original forms.
Man has made new varieties of the horse,
of the pigeon, of the rose, — so distinct
that a naturalist from another planet
would describe them as different species,
— by the simple method of breeding
exclusively from the individuals which
happened to possess the characteristics
desired. In the formation of true species, the struggle for life takes the place
of man's selective action, with the result
that, while in the competition ill-favored
varieties are exterminated, those organisms possessing modifications beneficial
to themselves, those which are "fittest"
in the given environment, survive, and, as
in the case of cultivated plants and domes-
ticated animals, they perpetuate their pe-
culiarities until, in the course of many
generations, there emerges the result of
new and distinct species.

Such is the essence of Darwinism, or
the doctrine of the origin of species. Like
all great and fruitful theories, it is simple
enough when once pointed out. Every
naturalist was already familiar with the
facts of variability, of the struggle for
existence, of adaptation to environment,

and of the inheritance of parental characteristics. But no one before Darwin suspected that, by a new collocation of these well-known phenomena, a scientific solution might be found for the mysterious problem of the origination of species. In a short time the leaders, and before long the rank and file, of zoölogists, botanists, and palæontologists accepted the Darwinian doctrine, at least as a working hypothesis. The only alternative was the belief in the creation of species; but as the Creator is the first cause of all things, and science seeks second or intermediary or natural causes, it was really no scientific explanation to say that species were created. Darwinism assumed no causes but such as could be proved to be actually at work. It had, therefore, the essential requisite of every scientific hypothesis. Whether it was adequate to explain the fact of the rise of species was another matter. And, for one, Huxley, while accepting the hypothesis, showed that its logical foundation was incomplete so long as the varieties produced by selective breeding were, while true species were not, more or less fertile with one another.

It is not for me to express an opinion on the validity of the Darwinian theory. I suppose, however, that no naturalist would now deny that *within certain limits* new species are originated by the survival and consolidation of such variations, spontaneously arising in organisms, as may be useful to their possessors in the struggle for life. Assuming, therefore, Darwinism to be true, I trust I may be permitted to observe that the origin of species remains almost as much a mystery as ever, though the mystery has been thrown a stage further back. Organisms differentiating themselves continuously along particular lines for indefinite periods of time must, under the law of the survival of the fittest, infallibly give rise to new species. But pray observe that *the survival of the fittest does not account for the arrival of the fittest.* That self-evolving organism, on which the entire issue is dependent, is a miracle which no naturalist has as yet transmuted into science. Natural Selection — a struggle for life and survival of the fittest — simply sifts the material furnished by the variability of plants and animals. The question then arises by what agency those variations are originated, shaped, and continued so that they are capable of producing those specific forms which, under the sifting of natural selection, actually emerge. Darwin himself was not insensible to the heavy weight of this unexplained mystery. In a letter to Huxley, written November 25, 1859, he expressed his perplexity concisely and aptly, though somewhat profanely, in the following query: "What the devil determines each particular variation? What makes a tuft of feathers come on a cock's head, or moss on a moss-rose?" If Darwin explained the appearance of new species, he did not explain the emergence of this differentiation of the organism — much less the origin of the organism itself — from which new species take their rise. The "Origin of Species" is, in fact, not the Genesis but the Exodus of living forms. It tells how a chosen seed, having been led out of the house of bondage,— the bondage to ancestral type,— waged a long struggle against the inhospitality of its environment and the attacks of its rivals, until at length it reached the promised goal,— the stature of an independent race, the transmutation into a new species.

One thing, however, is indisputable. The Darwinian hypothesis clearly belonged to the realm of science. If ever there was a passionless and abstract theory, Darwin's doctrine of the origination of species would seem to have deserved that characterization. And certainly no one but a master in the biological sciences should have presumed to estimate the validity, or fix the limits, of a theory resting on such a mass of observations, and sustained by so many lines of converging evidence, as those which Darwin brought to the support of the theory of Natural Selection. But oftenest the unexpected happens, — and this time the unwarranted. The ignorance, bigotry, and blind passion of the mob who condemned Socrates now took the judgment-seat for the hearing of Darwin. Dragged from the study and the laboratory into the garish light of public notoriety, his scientific hypothesis became the scandal of parlors and the ridicule of clubs, while press, platform, and pulpit thundered with a confused turmoil of refutation and invective, in which were mingled outrageous denunciations of the simple naturalist himself as a dangerous, godless, and even de-

generate member of the human species.
But if unthinking orthodoxy and prim pro-
priety were horrified, free-thinking radicalism went mad with delight. She wildly
clasped Darwinism to her bosom as the
hopeful parent of infidelity, materialism,
and atheism. What with friends and foes,
the plain craft of science had never before
got between such a Scylla and Charybdis!

But why all this public interest in the
new theory of organic species, you will ask ?
The mass of people, we all know, are not
as a rule much concerned about abstract
inquiries. Quite true; and I will say at
once that it was not Darwin's theory of the
origin of species which convulsed society,
but the inferences, deductions, and associated ideas which that theory suggested
concerning matters of vital and permanent
interest to humanity. (Human reason declares that God is the ground of the universe, and the moral and religious sense
gives assurance that He is the Father of our
spirits. Now this primary belief,— "in the
beginning, God,"— this datum of consciousness as I may call it, has, in the lapse
of many Christian centuries, become inseparably entwined with a venerable tradition

of creation, according to which species were instantaneously originated, immutably fixed, and permanently distinguished. Read once more the beautiful legend with which the Bible opens, — a legend so poetically vivid that Darwin's contemporaries still took it for history, as men devoid of culture and literary feeling do to this day, — read this story, I repeat, and you will see that the writer conceives of the species of plants and animals as sudden and unchangeable creations, with metes and bounds for each, and an impassable chasm between man and every other species. This legendary account of the genesis of things had, unfortunately, embosomed itself, not only in theology, but in the religious thought and feeling of Christendom. And when the " Origin of Species " appeared, the church had not yet recovered from the rude shock administered to the orthodox belief in impulsive creations by the uniformitarian geology of Lyell's "Principles." In sheer self-defence, therefore, religious minds felt impelled to attack the evolutionary biology which Darwin proclaimed and, still more, the revolutionary anthropology which loomed up behind it. If species were not immutable,

if related species were co-descendants of
the same ancestors, then man and the apes
— oh, unutterable horror! You smile at
the mention, or even at the suggestion, of
the pithecoid origin of mankind! But it
was a stone of stumbling to able and devout men of the last generation. What,
they asked, would become of the soul, of
sin, of the atonement, — nay, of the Creator
Himself thus discharged of so much of
the activity hitherto imposed upon Him?
It was, indeed, an awful crisis of thought.
And the travail and pathos of it will
long be remembered. But you who look
back on it, as to a remote period, with
the fresh eyes of youth, will not miss
the comic by-play that mingled with the
tragedy. You will see society divided into
two heraldic camps, one battling for an
ancestor a little lower than the angels and
the other for an ancestor a little higher
than the apes. You will see cool men lose
their heads, and men of good breeding part
with their manners, and men not hitherto
conspicuous for piety suddenly grown jeal-
ous about the honor of the Lord of Hosts.
And all the while it is forgotten that man
is what he is howsoever he came to be what

he is, and that in God all things live and move and have their being, though His children are forever misreading the way in which He does His wondrous works.

It was all over with science! In this fierce and indiscriminate polemic, the Darwinian hypothesis retreated from view before the spectres which it had evoked in the imagination of the excited disputants and the terrified public. The theory of the origination of species by natural selection was a generalization addressed to naturalists; but instead of receiving a dispassionate examination at the hands of experts, it became the occasion of a free fight over the entire area of that No Man's Land which lies between modern Science and traditional Theology. One party appealed to the sure word of revelation, the other to the inerrant record of nature. The points of issue were not clearly defined; their number multiplied as the bitterness of the disputants increased; and in time Darwinism became identified with a mass of biological, psychological, ethical, metaphysical, and theological speculations, having little or nothing in common but a genetic or historical method of treatment, and a content marked by opposition to current belief and orthodox Christianity.

Huxley at an early stage descended into this arena with alacrity and keen delight. Darwin gave him the sobriquet of " My General Agent." He became the leader of the radical hosts. While retaining his speculative doubt of Darwin's biological hypothesis, he was the head and front of the Darwinians. I have already described his splendid controversial powers; I may say here that he was too good a debater, too intense a partisan, too strong a hater, to put himself sympathetically at the standpoint of his opponents, and lead them by kindly tact and timely suggestion of higher truth out of the bondage of error in which he believed them benighted captives. His militant spirit was too strong for his pedagogical instinct. His genius was not constructive, but iconoclastic. He delighted to dare, to defy, to destroy; in dealing with persons not of his way of thinking, his aim was less instruction than refutation; and I suppose nothing gave him greater pleasure than to cleave an antagonist with the sword of his logic, unless it was to bewilder him with the rapier of his irony. I do not, of course, mean to disparage the value of discussion. My point is merely that, if Huxley could have had more sympathy with the Philistines, his arguments, though losing something of their point and dash, would have gained in illumination, efficacy, and fruitfulness. But one must take him as he was; and it was the nature of his analytic genius to revel in antinomies, and the method of his debate was to impale antagonists between the horns of an "either — or." Let us, however, not forget that besides the thesis and antithesis of the controversialist, there is the synthesis of the comprehensive thinker, and that the "either — or" of angry debate is often cancelled by the "both — and" of calm reflection. Whether the issues between Huxley and his adversaries may be so resolved, we must now proceed to consider.

I think that the many litigious suits in which Huxley was engaged as advocate for natural knowledge may all be embraced in three categories, which, though related, we may nevertheless clearly distinguish. First of all, there is the case of Science *versus* Revelation; secondly, the case of Evolution *versus* Creation; and, thirdly, the case of Pithecus or the Ape *versus* Adam. The first of these cases engrossed the latter years of his life; the other two claimed his attention at the outbreak of the war over Darwinism. The three, taken together, afforded abundant scope for the exhibition of that mental attitude which Huxley first designated Agnosticism. And though his creed as an Agnostic was not exhausted either in idea or in fact by his views on these disputed points, these were the only aspects of it which he ever fully developed, or in which he seemed sincerely and intensely interested. I shall have to allude to other elements of the Agnostic faith hereafter. Meantime let us see how the eponymous Agnostic filled his rôle in those vital contests between popular belief and evolutionary science to which I have just referred. It will be convenient to begin with the case of Evolution *versus* Creation.

That God is the ultimate ground and source of all things, whether they be living or inert, thinking or unthinking, seems to me not merely a conclusion reached by reflection and inference, but an intuitive belief constitutive of intelligence itself. Man, because he is rational, must believe in God as Universal First Cause ; atheism is, in the strictest sense of the term, irrational. Science, however, is in quest, not of the ultimate ground and reason of existence, but of the so-called secondary causes, — the proximate agencies and circumstances, — by which things have been modified in the natural order of events. It is, therefore, not an explanation of the scientific order to say that species of animals and plants were created by God. The proposition may be perfectly true and yet, in connection with science, totally irrelevant. What the biologist seeks to discover is the sequence of the natural phenomena by which it has been brought about that species have become what they are. And for the definite purpose, the limited inquiry, which science sets before itself as the goal of its endeavor, it matters not — I say it with no feeling of irreverence — whether there be a Creator or not. If proximate causes, if natural agencies, cannot be found to account for the origination of species, the problem for the man of science is unsolved, and it may be insoluble; but in any event, the case is not helped from the scientific point of view by the theory of supernatural creation. If it be true that all kinds of life came into existence instantaneously, by the mere fiat of the Divine Will, then this fact, instead of affording an alternative explanation to the biologist, carries the problem which he had raised out of the field of science altogether. Science stops where the sequence of natural events in time is broken by a supernatural occurrence. Science is simply the record of the behavior of things under the established order; neither her method nor her apparatus enables her to go beyond these limits; and when Omnipotence comes upon the scene, she is smitten with impotence. Only there are such good reasons for faith in the continuity of natural causation that no one can be expected to believe, without the strongest evidence, in a breach due to the miracle of supernatural agency.

How, then, stands the case with the origination of species? Men of science may be prejudiced in favor of an explanation by

natural causation, for it is their business
to seek secondary causes; but if, as a
matter of fact, species were miraculously
and instantaneously created by God, there
would be nothing for biology to do but to
accept the fact and confine its inquiries to
the behavior of the organisms which had
thus come supernaturally upon the field.
But we do not know that living forms
were thus originated. It was, no doubt,
the universal belief before Darwin. But
that belief had no other basis than the biblical account of creation; and we have now
learned that, whatever else the Bible may
do for us, it was never intended to teach
us science. Indeed the very conception of
science — derived, as it is, from the Greeks
— was foreign to the Hebrew mind. If
you read the Old Testament with the
slightest degree of attention, you will see
that none of the writers has any notion of
that order of nature and system of secondary causes which it is the function
of science to interpret. On the contrary,
they conceive of God as the direct and
immediate cause of all natural phenomena.
"The God of glory thundereth;" "the
voice of the Lord breaketh the cedars;"

" the voice of the Lord shaketh the wilderness ; " " the voice of the Lord maketh the hinds to calve ; " " the Lord sitteth upon the flood ; yea, the Lord sitteth King forever." These quotations are from a psalmist, it is true ; but neither in poet or prophet, chronicler or historian, will you discover any hint of nature as an intermediary system of relatively independent agencies ; and, the more fervid the inspiration of the writer, the more intensely does he picture all sublunary changes as doings of the Lord of Hosts. Ultimately considered, this interpretation seems to me to be true, eternally true. But it is a verity with which science has no concern. On the other hand, as I have said already, the Hebrew race had no genius for that exact and systematic knowledge of natural phenomena which is the desideratum of the scientific inquirer. When, therefore, this profound, but unscientific, people began to brood over the mysterious problem of the origin of things, they grasped, with a clearness that has never been excelled, the great and precious truth that God is the creative source of the world ; but when they proceeded to describe the procession of natural phenomena — the breaking of light on chaos, the formation of the globe, and the appearance of living creatures, "each after his kind"— they were so far from anticipating the discoveries of modern science that their only aim was to adorn the truth of reason with the poetry of a naive but sublime phantasy, for which they sketched a succession of pictures which still have potency to subdue the imagination and attune the emotions like the stately overture to an oratorio.

It is perfectly obvious to-day — or it should be — that if you would know the history of organisms you must consult the testimony of the fossiliferous rocks. It was very different when Huxley began his investigations. Everybody then supposed it was enough to consult the Book of Genesis. It became Huxley's duty, as a man of science, to show that the two records did not agree. And he accomplished the task, which it must be owned he found far from uncongenial, with an array of evidence and a cogency of demonstration which convinced everybody except his discomfited antagonists and the invincible torturers of the Hebrew text. Huxley professed to have a perfectly open mind towards the two records, to have no prejudice one way or the other; and he declared that the view which he accepted was commended solely by the conclusiveness of the evidence in its favor. Perhaps he deceived himself; perhaps he was influenced, to some extent, at least, by his way of looking at things in general — what Mr. Balfour has since called the "psychological climate." But Huxley was certainly not conscious of any such distracting cause of belief. In relation to the conflict between the creational and the evolutional doctrine of the origin of species, he conceived his mind as a freely acting balance, which, however moved, was moved solely by the weight of the evidence adduced. And this hospitality and loyalty of the mind to evidence, with the putting away of authority, tradition, and every other circumstance, is what Huxley means by the Agnosticism of the man of science.

I have hitherto spoken of the case of Evolution *versus* Creation solely from the point of view of biology. Huxley's contention is that, as concerns the time, order, and manner in which living kinds came into existence, the stratified rocks tell one story and the Book of Genesis another. But Huxley (putting aside the colossal blunder of Bathybius, which he frankly acknowledged) has nothing to say of the first beginning of those primordial species from whose varieties other species may subsequently have been formed. And, of course, as a biologist, he was under no temptation to account for the origin of the inorganic world or of the realm of conscious minds. It is conceivable, indeed, that the universe is eternal; but, if so, reflection shows that neither now nor at any other moment could it exist without the sustaining energy of the Divine Volition; and Goethe finely calls it "the living garment of God." But, however it be with the universe, it is a certainty of science that at one time there was neither life nor consciousness on this globe. To the man of science their emergence must be a miracle, for it is a violation of the law of natural causation. The religious mind calls it a creation. Evolutionary science would have accomplished its goal only if it could show that life had developed from inorganic matter, and mind from unconscious life. From the primitive nebula of the universe to man who knows it, the chain of evolution would then be complete. There would be no break in what Huxley described as "Nature's great progression, from the formless to the formed — from the inorganic to the organic — from blind force to conscious intellect and will." But science has not realized this ideal; and it is probably unrealizable. This is doubtless a great comfort to the general public. Were the realization ever achieved, many pious minds, who can see God only when He breaks in on the order of natural causation, would have to walk by faith; and I fear, in the absence of sight, the light would seem dim indeed. Yet a primitive chaos of star-dust, which held in its womb not only the cosmos that fills space, not only the living creatures that teem upon it, but also the intellect that interprets it, the will that confronts it, and the conscience that transfigures it, must as certainly have God at the centre as a universe mechanically arranged and periodically adjusted must have Him at the circumference. There is no real antagonism between Cre-

ation and Evolution. The notion of Creation implies the absolute beginning of
existence; the notion of Evolution implies gradual and progressive change in
that which already exists. Creation is
not only in itself *toto cœlo* different from
Evolution; it is as much the prerequisite
of Evolution as your bodily system is of
digestion. Evolution is merely the mode
in which, according to modern science,
God manifests Himself alike in the world
of nature and in the world of spirit. His
procedure is not by spasms and cataclysms;
but here a little, there a little, and ever
gradually onward.

I wonder what posterity will make of
the confusion which the law of evolution
caused in the minds of the generation
which in the nineteenth century first
discovered conclusive evidence of its
operation ? They will surely learn with
amazement and incredulity that the discovery was in high quarters supposed to
be fatal to a belief in God, and that, what
in old times the fool had said in his heart,
was in that age proclaimed upon the house-
tops as the final inference of science and
philosophy. As though man's faith *that*

God is could be shaken by a new glimpse of *how God acts!* Surely it remains a necessary postulate of intelligence — a datum as reasonable and trustworthy as belief in the existence of anything whatsoever — that God is the creative source and sustaining ground of the universe, — and that, whether He poured forth His energy at a definite then and there, or, as I believe, continues to diffuse it through every point of infinite space and to maintain it at every moment of unending time.

I must do Huxley the justice of explaining that his clear intellect was never obscured by the delusion that atheism was an inference from the theory of evolution. What he attacked was that venerable tradition of the process of creation, which had been so long accepted as a part of religion itself; and he attacked it for the good and sufficient reason that it was at variance with the facts revealed in the fossiliferous strata of the earth's crust.

I have to some extent already touched upon Huxley's advocacy of the simian or pithecoid origin of man. I have designated this issue the case of Pithecus *versus* Adam. Huxley considered the issue one of capital importance. His own attitude brought upon him criticism and ridicule, and not only those, but also animadversion and reproof; and for a time, as he long afterwards good-naturedly said, he was little better than one of the wicked. But Huxley needed opposition; he liked fighting; and this crusade was in the cause of truth. Indeed it is difficult to know how a fair-minded and honest biologist who saw so far could have forborne to say as much as Huxley set down in his famous pamphlet on "Man's Place in Nature." Science must needs be truthful, outright, and downright. And Huxley was not the man to make his biographer blush, as Bacon had made Macaulay blush " for the disingenuousness of the most devoted worshipper of speculative truth, for the servility of the boldest champion of intellectual freedom." Herein Huxley is an admirable example to every student and thinker. The thing that is true may not be welcome — for interests are entrenched behind what is current; but if you know it to be true — I am not speaking of guessing but of knowledge, and I say if you are sure you have ascertained the truth, in God's name speak it out and keep not silent! This is what Huxley did in regard to the question of man's relation to the animals next below him. Even before the appearance of "The Origin of Species" he had thought much of the structural affinities of men and apes ; and the views at which he had arrived were in full harmony with those which Darwin now proclaimed. "Man's Place in Nature" was finished in 1862. Taking account both of fœtal development and adult structure, this work demonstrated the most striking similarities between man and the man-like apes. In the processes of origination, in the early stages of formation, in the mode of nutrition before and after birth, man's history is identical with that of the apes; and in his developed structure the resemblances with theirs are as striking as they are fundamental. After comparing their several organs with great care and exactitude, Huxley reached the conclusion that the structural differences which separate man from the gorilla and the chimpanzee are not so great as those which separate the gorilla from the lower apes. And this leads directly to the conclusion which so horrified Huxley's generation. If animals of similar structure and function are ever descended from common ancestors, then there is no rational ground for doubting, either that the human species might have originated by differentiation from the simian, or that both are modified ramifications of a common ancestral stock. Now Darwin's investigations prove that species do, sometimes at any rate, originate through modifications in the co-descendants of common ancestors. Accordingly, Huxley regarded the simian origin of man as highly probable. And it afforded intense satisfaction to his craving for scientific explanation to be able to trace the condition of the entire organic world, as Lyell had traced that of the inorganic, to the efficiency of causes still operating about us.

There is, as I have already intimated, a feeling — I think I may say a conviction — among scientists of the present day that the Darwinian theory of descent with modifications has been pushed too far, and that corollaries have been drawn from it which a longer and more accurate acquaintance with the facts shows to be altogether unwarranted. Something like a reaction from earlier Darwinism seems now in full force. In time the limits of the new truth will be defined. Meanwhile we are in doubt and uncertainty. In striking contrast is Darwin's own assurance' of man's descent from the lower animals. In the postscript to a letter to Lyell, written as early as January, 1850, he tells his friend that he has a "pleasant genealogy for mankind"; and describes our remotest ancestor as an "animal which breathed water, had a swim-bladder, a great swimming tail, an imperfect skull, and was undoubtedly an hermaphrodite!"

Be it so! Yet

"A man's a man for a' that."

If at the beginning he starts with the brute, and if at the end his body may return to the basest uses, still 'twere to consider too curiously to consider so, unless we also observed that this quintessence of dust is not only the paragon of animals, but the one self-conscious denizen of our world, noble in reason, infinite in faculty, in action like an angel, in apprehension like a God. Assume, I say, that Darwin's "pleasant genealogy for mankind" should pass muster with the herald's college of contemporary biology. What matters it that you have come from brutishness, if you are come to humanity? What matters it that your ancestor was an ape, if you are a man? I ask not what you are derived from, but what you have arrived at? The vital matter is not whether a man started at this point or at that, but, in the expressive slang of our day, whether he "got there." If you are conscious of the dignity and responsibility of human living, you will survey with indifference speculations concerning the origin of your race, knowing that you are not one whit the better or the worse whether it started with a fallen archangel or an exalted ape. Of course Lady Clara Vere de Vere might see peril to her "hundred coats-of-arms." But that in a democratic community like ours, where worth and not birth is the test of manhood, there should be an aversion to

Darwin's doctrine of the descent of man as degrading to humanity, is a curious illustration of the tenacity with which sentiments survive the institutions and beliefs which made them appropriate, and live on even when they have become irrational and absurd. If men are to be judged, not by what they are, but by what they came from, not only biology, not only science, but common experience as well will force us to a complete revision of our estimate of mankind. If any one of us could trace his pedigree through a hundred generations, he would find at the other end a naked savage but little removed from the brutes. Nay, a short time ago and you yourself were merely a germ which no ordinary power of discrimination could distinguish from an incipient puppy. But these facts are neither degrading nor brutalizing to your humanity. They put on you no obligation to scalp your neighbors, or to grovel on all fours. You are — *not what you have come from*, but *what you have become*. And the knowledge of your lowly beginnings should give you faith and hope in your capacity for still higher things.

There may be atavism, there may be reversion to primitive types; but the general tendency of evolution being to fuller and better life, it is assuredly the destiny of man to

> "Move upward, working out the beast,
> And let the ape and tiger die."

No one knew this better than Huxley. Asserting, on the one hand, that no absolute line of demarcation could be drawn between the structure of man and the structure of the animals next below him, and holding that even the highest faculties of the human mind begin to germinate in lower forms of life, the evolutionary biologist was also profoundly conscious of the vastness of the gulf between civilized man and the brutes, and he declared, in felicitous and striking terms, that "whether *from* them or not, man is assuredly not *of* them." This Agnosticism does not touch the dignity or the spiritual vocation of man. True, Huxley did not, as he aptly put it, "base man's dignity upon his great toe, or insinuate that we are lost if an ape has a hippocampus minor." What he did was to raise a simple question of fact, namely, whether the human species did not strongly resemble the simian, and to suggest an explanation, namely, whether they might not have had a common origin. This is the meaning of Huxley's Agnosticism in relation to the question of the origin of man. At this distance of time nothing could seem more harmless or less disquieting.

I have now examined the case of Evolution *versus* Creation and the case of Pithecus *versus* Adam. There remains, to complete our survey of the Agnosticism developed by Huxley, the case of Science *versus* Revelation. This issue I have to some extent already anticipated. The conflict between the evolutional and the creational theories of the origin of living beings, and particularly of man, is a part — and a part of great strategic importance — of the general warfare between Science and Revelation. To this comprehensive issue itself I now briefly invite your attention.

As ordinarily understood, Revelation gives us inerrant truth on infallible authority. Science yields provisional theories with no better warrant than uncontradicted experience. At first sight Revelation might seem to be the more fruitful and trustworthy source of knowledge; and the ages of faith so regarded it. But ours is an epoch of criticism. We demand the grounds of belief; we suffer no claims to pass on the plea of their sanctity or of their antiquity. In this work of criticism, the one sure standard is experience. I use the word "experience" in the broadest possible sense; and I say that the age of science which has supervened upon the age of faith holds the experience of mankind to be the best and safest test of truth. We are not, however, justified in rejecting everything that transcends the range of ordinary human experience. On the contrary, so far as we know, to-morrow may produce events which yesterday would have been miracles. It is not criticism, it is not science, but it is dogmatism of the most arrant type, to assert that miracles are impossible. What then should be the intellectual attitude of the candid inquirer in regard to assertions of miraculous occurrences which claim to be the sure word of Revelation — inerrant truth on infallible authority? I answer unhesitatingly that, before giving his assent to those statements, such an inquirer must satisfy himself, first, that there is evidence sufficient to show that the events in question actually happened, and, secondly, that their occurrence is insusceptible of explanation on natural grounds. This would involve a close scrutiny of all the facts and circumstances in connection with every reported miracle, for the purpose of ascertaining the evidential value of the whole. Nor would this be the end of the inquiry. Besides this specific examination in each case, it would be necessary to make a general canvass of the claims of Revelation as resting on infallible authority and furnishing inerrant truth. Appeals to antiquity, to authority, to tradition would have no more weight in the settlement of the question than a fair-minded judge might consider the equitable due of ancient times, illustrious names, and sayings generally received.

I say, then, that the miraculous occurrences recorded in the Bible must be subjected to those tests before any critical inquirer can be asked to accept or reject them.

Of course the natural events described by
the sacred writers will be judged by the
ordinary canons of historic credibility.
In the light of these criteria, we may now
ask what attitude our Agnostic scientist
assumed in relation to the claims of Revelation. I can, I think, describe his position in a very few words. In the first
place, Huxley finds that, while in some
cases the sacred books of Revelation declare that certain events happened in a
certain fashion, the secular books of Science prove that they did not. And, in
the second place, Huxley finds that while,
in other cases, the wonderful statements
of the Bible are not contradicted by Science, they are not supported by inherent
evidence sufficient to make them probable
or credible. The total result is, both as
regards historical events and supranatural
occurrences, that the same liability to
error and the same intrinsic improbabil-
ity which we so readily recognize in the
narratives of the sacred books of other
peoples become the portion of our own
Bible, which had hitherto, in almost universal estimation, been set apart by the
notes of canonicity, inerrancy, and author-

ity.   Huxley bases his conclusion on an
examination of typical specimens of the
Old Testament and the New; and in making his selections he showed a marked and
constant predilection for what he called
the "Noachian Deluge" and "the Bedevilment of the Gadarene Swine." For insistence on fact, for force of reasoning, for
lucidity of style, for the unconventional
way in which he treats theological subjects, for disregard of everything but
what he believed the evidence in the
case, and for the radical character of his
results, Huxley, in these writings, was unparalleled in his generation and in recent
times finds a parallel in Strauss alone.   I
may add, too, that the very general ap-
proval which the intelligent public ac-
corded to Huxley's excursions into the
realm of theology shows that the English-speaking world had already entered
into a new era of thought and culture —
a critical era in which the barriers between
theology and reason have been broken
down, and the most venerable dogmas
left to stand or fall with the evidence
adduced to support them.

Of course, the Bible contains myth and

legend, allegory and fable, poetry and prose; and it ought not to be surprising that critical science — historical and physical — should discover errors in the sensuous setting of the supersensuous spiritual truth and life it was intended to reveal. Grant that none of the miracles reported in the Old Testament occurred, grant that many of the historical events were very different from what the records would naturally lead us to suppose; still Israel's vision of a reign of righteousness on earth and in heaven is to this day verified in the soul of every good man who studies their laws and maxims or who communes with their psalmists and their prophets. Or look at the New Testament. What if the "Bedevilment of the Gadarene Swine," which proved such a stumbling-block to Huxley, never took place; what if all the miraculous occurrences in the natural world recorded in the Gospels were the fantastic tribute of a pious generation, unskilled in the art of writing history and ignorant of the constancy of nature's laws, to a transcendent personality who commanded their loyalty, touched all the springs of their affection, and thrilled their

E

souls with a consuming sense of the inalien-
able and indefeasible nearness of man to
God ?   Would not that miracle of miracles
still remain, — Jesus of Nazareth, the won-
der-worker of human history ?   And would
not the purpose of His coming — "I am
come that ye might have life and that
ye might have it more abundantly " — be
fulfilled in the revelation He made, not
only through His teachings but in His
human life, both of the actual fatherliness
of God and the potential divineness of
man ?   These are spiritual truths which
neither age can stale nor custom wither,
which no science can disprove and no
criticism discredit ; they are truths which
transcend both the order of nature and the
secular history of humanity ; yet truths
which, once revealed and incarnated by
the divine "Son of Man," approve themselves eternal verities to our religious
intuition and feeling — that divining intelligence

"Whose kingdom is where time and space are not."

I do not think that Christian faith
should be shaken or disturbed by new
interpretations of the Bible.   That the

essence of it is imperishable truth — truth of the spiritual order — the heart of man will perennially attest. Intrinsic falsity — what Plato called the lie in the soul — not even the veriest sceptic has asserted of the sacred writings. But we have this treasure of spiritual truth in " earthen vessels." The scenes in space and events in time which represent it to one age of culture may misrepresent it to another. In the lapse of ages the portrayal may become a caricature. Whenever such a crisis arrives, men become so absorbed in destroying the trappings of truth that they lose sight of the majestic figure these were intended to set off and decorate. Your destructive critic is forever missing the eternal essence of truth in his pursuit of the changeable and perishable forms of its embodiment. Cosmogonical legends, didactic chronicles, wonderful stories of non-natural occurrences in nature, served to convey spiritual truth to earlier and more ignorant generations of mankind. But in themselves these things are devoid of spiritual efficacy. They are merely the bells to call primitive peoples to church. Sweet as the music they once made, mod-

ern ears find them jangling and out of
tune; and their dissonant notes scare
away pious souls who would fain enter
the temple of worship. In the divinely
ordered education of the race, man has
progressed so far that he is now capable
of apprehending in its purity that spiritual truth which was set forth to earlier
generations in the forms of theophanies,
miracles, and extraordinary scenes and
occurrences. What the devout scholar
and the devout scientist of modern times
yearns for is, not the theology of Christendom, but the religion of Christ. That
religion I call the absolute religion. It
is not true because it is in the Bible; it is
in the Bible because it is eternally true.
Its forms may change; its embodiments
may perish; its records may pass away;
for all these belong to the world of sense
and may fall a prey to the contingencies of
time; but the religion which Jesus lived
and taught will endure as long as the
human soul itself, which it is the glory of
that religion to have bound indissolubly to
its Divine Original. The Christian religion, as a system of dogmatic theology, is
already obsolescent (even in the churches,

or in many of them, it is an alien and un-
heeded survival); but the religion of Christ
is still fresh with the dews of immortal
youth and pregnant with abounding life
to quicken the souls of all the children of
men. Throughout Christendom there has
been a recoil of men's minds from creed to
personality. The evolution of our religion brings us at the dawn of the twentieth
century back to Christ Himself.

It is at this point that Huxley's treatment of the Christian religion seems to
me especially unsatisfactory. Evolutionist
as he was, he overlooked the fact that both
Christianity and the interpretation of its
records are subject to the law of evolution.
Now in theology, as in other provinces of
inquiry, the idea of development has become the master light of all our seeing.
In a world where everything changes and
grows, where the mind of man enlarges,
we naturally look for new experiences of
religion, new conceptions of the Bible,
and new expositions of doctrine. These
changes are the phases of an evolving life,
and, rightly considered, they witness to
the inherent vitality of Christianity. If
creeds are shifting, it is only that they

may the better adjust themselves to that more correct interpretation of God's revelation to and in man which in the progress of the ages the human mind is continuously attaining to. Such a modification of creeds means the purification, simplification, and rejuvenation of Christian theology. But Huxley read such transformations of dogma as the annihilation of theology. As though a man must repudiate Christianity because unable to accept the creed of his grandmother! Huxley was led into this absurdity by the assumption (utterly foreign though it is to the spirit of modern scholarship) that if the Bible be not history, — a literal record and chronicle of events which actually happened, — it is not possible for us to have a Christian theology or, if I understand him aright, even a Christian religion. A Christianity independent of time and place, eternally true, and verified by every soul that finds it and which it finds, — a spiritual religion as indifferent to history as it is to science, transcending both, and holding the high places of the human spirit; this is something Huxley never dreamt of. Christianity must be

"historical" in all its details or it is —
illusion! Nay, "Christian theology," he
tells us in the controversial essay on "The
Lights of the Church and the Light of Science," "must stand or fall with the historical trustworthiness of the Jewish Script-
ures." It is all up with Christianity, if
those definite and detailed Old Testament
narratives of apparently real events are not
actually historical, — if the covenant with
Abraham was not made, if circumcision
was not ordained by Jehovah, if the deca-
logue was not written by God's hand on
the stone tables, if Abraham is more or less
a mythical hero, the story of the deluge a
fiction, that of the fall a legend, and that
of creation the dream of a seer! One
would ordinarily say that, if these events
are not historical, there is room in that
great collection of books we call the Bible
for other and higher forms of literary expression than the sober chronicle of the
historian; and that the truths of poetry,
parable, and legend may be more important
and fruitful for constructive theology than
the truths of history. Not so Huxley.
He will have nothing but history. And
turning, in the essay on "Agnosticism and

Christianity," to the New Testament, he lays bare its unhistorical features by dissecting the story of the Gadarene swine, demonstrating its incredibility, and consequently bringing under suspicion all other stories of demoniac possession. But if the "demonological part of Christianity" be rejected, Huxley holds that the testimony of Jesus, who accepted that demonology, to the spiritual world — His declaration of the personality, fatherhood, and loving providence of God — will have been profoundly impaired, if it is not indeed rendered absolutely valueless. As Huxley put it in his rejoinder to Gladstone, entitled "The Keepers of the Herd of Swine," "the authority of the teachings of the Synoptic Gospels, touching the nature of the spiritual world, turns upon the acceptance, or the rejection, of the Gadarene and other like stories."

It is humiliating to think that the wretched pigs of Gadara may make or unmake our religious faith. For my own part, I cannot for a moment assent to such a view. And I have already acquainted you with some of the grounds which compel me to reject it. I will here only illustrate my position by a reference to that book which men and women of English speech are in the habit of mentioning next after the Bible — I mean, of course, the dramas of Shakespeare. Let me ask you to consider for a moment two of those plays, — "Hamlet" and "Macbeth." In these dramas the actors are not all human beings; witches and ghosts come upon the scene; and to Shakespeare and his contemporaries these supernatural entities were (I presume) as real as the mundane characters. We have lost man's primitive faith in the existence of ghosts and witches. But "Hamlet" and "Macbeth" are as true and significant to us as they were to Shakespeare's contemporaries. As a revelation of the depths of human nature — of a soaring intellect and a paralyzed will, of the lust of power and an imagination that dallies with it while painting also the pangs of remorse — these plays have a worth and also a vitality unaffected by the place or time of their production, or even by the perishable elements entering into their composition. And you will not fail to note either that our estimation of the value of these plays, our appreciation of their meaning, and our participation in the author's insight are absolutely independent of any theories that may be formed concerning the life and character of Shakespeare. Indeed, while the dramas are the immortal heritage of our race, we know next to nothing of the dramatist.

In the same way I apprehend that, if the Bible were annihilated, the religion of Christ would be approved and verified by the religious consciousness of Christendom. It was revealed that it might be received of men, and the historical revelation has now (may I not say?) become the ideal possession of the human spirit.

I think Huxley himself in his later years got a glimpse of the truth that the conflict between Science and Revelation was to be settled by the development of both. He came to recognize a certain class of inquirers as " scientific theologians," whom he opposed to " counsels for creeds " — the advocates of " Clericalism " and " Ecclesiasticism." Those theologians he called " scientific," because they based their assertions, not on authority, but on evidence. Here the theologian and the scientist occupied common ground.

And Huxley could and did appreciate it. But I do not think Huxley ever recognized how much Revelation contained, and must contain, other than propositions addressed to the intellect. Its peculiar field is the emotions, and more particularly the moral and spiritual nature of man. In this field the watchword is not evidence, but inspiration; the aim is not truth, but higher life. Huxley, with the fine frenzy for "natural knowledge" that possessed him throughout all his work and controversy, never realized how much of what is best in life lies outside that restricted territory. He sought, very properly, to expel from belief improbable stories of supernatural occurrences amid the regular flow of natural events; but he never rose to the full height of the argument from which he might have surveyed natural causation as the expression of a Supernatural Mind in nature, and man — a being at once of sensibility and of rational and moral self-activity — as a signal and ever-present example of the interfusion of the natural with the supernatural in that part of universal existence nearest and best known to us.

I have discussed this problem at too
great length, and I must now hasten on.
There remain two forms of Agnosticism
yet to be mentioned in any adequate account of Huxley.   One of them we may
call Metaphysical and the other Logical
Agnosticism.   The former I must dismiss
with a word.   Huxley often alludes to it,
but never attempts to establish or develop
it.   It is the dogma — the colossal dogma
— that the human mind is incapable of
apprehending God.   A man who can in-
telligently frame that proposition should
be called not agnostic, but omniscient.
For the doctrine means that God is of
such a nature, and the human mind of
such a make, that the two can never come
together.   Huxley picked up the tenet
from an essay of Sir William Hamilton,
which he read as a boy.   And his boyish
credulity remained with him to the end
of his days.   I have elsewhere [1] examined
the doctrine, and must here content my-
self with categorically rejecting it as " not
proven."   That the human mind is incapable of knowing anything of God, is a
dogma that rests on no evidence whatever.

[1] See the next chapter.

The man who propounds it, whatever he may call himself, is the greatest dogmatist the world has ever seen. The philosophers who first set it forth deduced it from the premises — the false premises — which they inherited from one-sided systems of thought. In Hume, it flows from an absurd sensationalism, in Kant, from an equally absurd rationalism, — both of them now happily obsolete. And Hume and Kant are the authorities whom Huxley invokes to support his theological nescience !

The only remaining phase of Agnosticism is what I have called Logical Agnosticism. This is not a creed of any kind, either positive or negative ; it asserts no tenet, and· denies none; it connotes an attitude of mind in dealing with evidence, " which is as much ethical as intellectual." It signifies candor, open-mindedness, and a resolute determination to believe what the facts warrant, neither more nor less. The doctrine that there are propositions which men ought to believe without logically satisfactory evidence, or (in Dr. Newman's words) that " religious error is, in itself, of an immoral nature," is abhorrent and shocking to the Agnostic. Agnosticism, in this sense, is synonymous with scientific method applied to every realm of inquiry. You will find Agnostics in literature, history, theology, philosophy, and science. They bring existing beliefs to the test of fact, with the result of suspending, altering, or confirming our judgment of their validity. The Agnostic is a judge weighing evidence, a critic balancing conflicting probabilities.

This phase of Agnosticism is that in which Huxley delighted as a champion of intellectual liberty. With an air of superiority, perhaps pardonable under the circumstances, he would fling it in the teeth of his creed-bound opponent, as though thanking God (if only there were a God) that he was not as other men or even as this poor "ecclesiastic." But the fact is that Huxley missed the real point of difference between himself and the " ecclesiastic." Both of them appeal alike to evidence ; both reason on the facts of the case in dispute. What distinguishes them is that the sort of evidence which convinces one, leaves the mind of the other unmoved. Their methods are the same ;

they are both scientific, critical, or (if you will) agnostic ; and if they reach entirely different results, it is because the unexpressed premises of their reasonings are different and perhaps contradictory. The fundamental assumptions that shape and color all thinking, the psychological climate in which the intellect lives and works, the primal elements of character which remain below the threshold of consciousness, — these influence all our beliefs and reasonings, and in a Huxley and a Gladstone they present as wide diversities as any of the contrary theories these distinguished advocates ever espoused. Think, for example, of the impossibility of two intelligent, candid, and critical inquirers reaching similar conclusions on some religious dogma, when the bias, native or acquired, of the one mind is towards scientific naturalism, and that of the other towards ecclesiastical supranaturalism.

If, however, Huxley meant by Agnosticism the adoption of the scientific spirit and method, there is no investigator or thinker, whatever his creed, who would not to-day write himself down an Agnostic.   One gets the impression, however, that Huxley's Agnostic must also be hostile to conventional Christianity.   On this latter point I have already spoken to you, and I have no time here to enlarge upon the theme.   As to the main issue now before us, I will only repeat that if Agnosticism means merely the candid examination and criticism of evidence, there is no one in this scientific age of the world who would disavow, no one who would not glory in, the title of Agnostic.

To Agnosticism, in its various forms, Huxley may be said to have consecrated his life.   In one of his latest pieces of writing, — in the preface to the " Collected Essays," in nine volumes, which happily he lived long enough to see through the press, — he has put on record the main objects of his active career.   They were, in brief, veracity of thought and action, the resolute facing of the world as it is, the unlocking of nature's secrets by means of science, and the application of scientific methods of investigation to all the problems of life.   If he showed untiring opposition to clericalism, to the spirit of ecclesiasticism, it was because everywhere and to whatever denomination it may belong, he regarded it as "the deadly enemy of science."

Few men, I imagine, have ever attained more fully the objects of their ambition. Huxley was the great enemy of cant, lying, and pretending to believe that for which there is no evidence. For this all honest men owe him a debt of gratitude. He earned the praise of every investigator, scholar, and thinker by his splendid vindication of intellectual liberty. And even theologians (of the future, if not of the present) may bless him for exposing the absurdities of many dogmas which were yesterday a part of orthodox Christianity, which to-day — thanks in some measure to Huxley — have lost their baneful energy, and which, dissolved in the light of criticism, will to-morrow flit to that limbo of superstitions, errors, and illusions which fill so many volumes in the history of our groping race.

All honor and glory to this brilliant champion of light, and liberty, and truth ! He saw clearly, studied thoroughly, and spoke boldly.

F

Yet Huxley had his limitations. His horizon was restricted to his field of labor: he saw the natural world, but not the supranatural which envelops it. His hand was subdued to what it worked in : he grasped the judgments of the intellect, but missed the intimations of the spirit in man. He lived in the laboratory and lecture room : no man knew more of the tests and standards of physical science, few men knew less of the postulates and principles of human conduct and life. Huxley's defects are his excellences in excess. He sees nature so thoroughly, uses his intellect so logically, and rates science so highly, that he falls a victim to the vices of Naturalism, Intellectualism, and what (for want of a better word) I will venture to call Scientificism.

I have already shown that evolutionary science furnishes no warrant for that naturalistic view of the universe which dominates all Huxley's speculations. Nay, one may be an Agnostic, as well as an Evolutionist, and yet recognize the divine and suprasensible Presence in and above the physical universe. I will explain what I mean by a comparison. Martineau would agree with Huxley in demanding evidence, instead of authority, for religious belief ; and, as Huxley uses the term, Martineau would therefore be an Agnostic. Nevertheless I venture to assert that no man now living has done so much to strengthen faith in a free moral intelligence immanent in, yet transcending, the natural world and holding communion with the finite but kindred spirits who inhabit it. As biblical critics, Huxley and Martineau occupy pretty much the same position; as spiritual influences, revealing the divine essence of things, the one radiates light and warmth for the English-speaking world, the other stands opaque and cold beside the extinguished fires of an altar to the unknown God.

But if Huxley's contentment with the mere physical interpretations of science was fatal to a theistic conception of the world, if his Naturalism left no place for the supersensuous and divine, his devotion to the ascertainment of truth by means of logical processes incapacitated him for taking a just view of the human spirit and foredoomed him to a narrow and one-sided Intellectualism. Knowl-

edge is only one of the functions of mind.
Mere intellectual assent or denial marks
but a small part of the essential life of
consciousness. If any of you have read
Disraeli's " Coningsby " you will recall the
striking passage in which Sidonia shows
how little reason has contributed to the
great ·events of human history. It was
not reason, he says, that besieged Troy ;
it was not reason that sent forth the Sara-
cen from the desert to conquer the world ;
it was not reason that inspired the Cru-
sader or instituted the monastic orders ;
it was not reason that created the French
Revolution. The true greatness of man
is to be found in his capacity for forming
and cherishing ideals. In this age of
brilliant scientific achievements issuing in
manifold conveniences and luxuries, I fear
we have all been seduced into worship-
ping the golden calf of Intellectualism.
It would ill become me, in this place and
before this audience, to disparage the
value of scientific investigation or to dis-
courage whole-hearted devotion to the
ascertainment of truth. But I cannot
forbear to observe that the spirit which
each of us is consists not of intellect or

reason alone. And this discernment of
the real constitution of human nature is
not without important consequences. For
one thing, it follows that the maxims
which are binding on the scientist in
the investigation of nature may be irrelevant or even injurious to the rest of mankind who are engaged in other affairs.
For the scientist, Huxley says, "scepticism is the highest of duties; blind faith
the one unpardonable sin." Now if this
be the duty of the scientist, it is not
the duty of the parent or child, of the
statesman or teacher, of the merchant or
manufacturer, of the clerk or financier.
Nay, has not every true man faith —
"blind faith" — in his mother and in his
friends, in his country, and in the rule
of Eternal Providence? It is, unhappily,
true that the scientist's devotion to "scepticism" may unfit him for living that
larger life which breathes the atmosphere
of faith. Darwin observed in his own
case an atrophy of the poetic and æsthetic
sensibilities; and readers of his life will
feel that his religious faith suffered decay
from the same cause. Cramping and
warping is the penalty of specialization

along whatever line it follow. But the
fact remains that for living our human
lives faith is as essential as scepticism,
nay, far more essential. It was his fail-
ure to comprehend the depths and riches
of the human spirit, whose logical operations alone concerned him as a scientist,
that led Huxley to the shrine of Intellectualism, whose creed, however fruitful for
science, becomes, if applied beyond the
domain of science, a desecration and blight
to the whole spiritual and active life of
humanity.

A few words on what I have called
Huxley's Scientificism, and I will bid you
good night. By this term I mean to
designate the astonishing prejudice that
the scientific investigator, the man who
has great knowledge of the natural world,
is, as such, an authority on the things of
the spirit. This is a prejudice which
indicates no self-conceit in Huxley; for
he shared it with the generations that
have grown up in the atmosphere of
modern science. We all want to know
what Darwin or Helmholtz or any other
oracle of the natural world thought of the
moral and spiritual problems which weigh

upon us. We find, however, through mournful disappointments, that they have little or nothing to tell us. They have had no special experience that way, if indeed their minds have not been closed to this order of reality. In consulting them our age has made the mistake of conferring with perhaps the worst-qualified exponents of the spiritual world to whom it was possible to address such inquiries. Mr. Gladstone has recently recorded it, as a generalization of his long experience with Englishmen of every class and type, that the description of persons who are engaged in political employment or who are in any way habitually conversant with human nature, conduct, and concerns are very much less borne down by scepticism than specialists of various kinds and those whose pursuits have associated them with the study, history, and framework of inanimate nature. How can this latter class be expected to tell us anything about that of which they have had no experience ? The oracle to consult in matters of religion is the man of faith and action, not the man of scepticism and science. His reports of the spiritual world, as verified in his own life, are entitled to the same weight as the observations, verified by artificial experiment, which the scientist reports of the natural world. If the one is our authority for scientific belief, the other is entitled to be our authority for religious faith. I will not here name our highest authority for belief and trust in God. It is enough that you address your inquiries to any man of action who allied himself with moral causes and worked for spiritual ends. I take at random a product of our own native soil.

Huxley says that Darwin was "the incorporated ideal of a man of science." I should say that Lincoln was the incorporated ideal of a man of action. Charles Darwin and Abraham Lincoln! These are the two greatest names of the century. The one wrought a revolution in natural science, the other in the affairs and institutions of his own country. There are strange coincidences in the lives of these two men. Both were born on the 12th day of February, 1809. The Englishman had the advantage of a refined home, a school and college education, travel and study abroad, and the leisure of a lifetime to meditate and write. Lincoln was born in a log-cabin in Kentucky, went to school for less than a year, worked as a common farm laborer till he became of age, and served afterwards as a boatman, a clerk, a storekeeper, a soldier, a postmaster, and a surveyor, until finally he became a lawyer and in 1834 was elected to the legislature of Illinois. For the next two decades Lincoln lived a comparatively uneventful life, not distinguishing himself above his contemporaries, and had he died before 1857 the world would never have heard his name. Throughout this same period Darwin, in studious retirement, unknown to the public, was chewing the cud of natural selection. At the same time both men were suddenly pushed into prominence and publicity, and had fame thrust upon them, by the action of illustrious rivals who threatened to pluck their foreordained honors. The inciting genius of the one was Wallace ; of the other, Douglas. Alike moved to action in 1858, Darwin published the first outline of a new theory of the origin of species, which was destined to put him at the head of modern science ; and Lincoln delivered his "divided house" speech, which made him two years later President of the United States.   .

Never before in the history of the world did a ruler come to so dubious and difficult an estate. The Republic was already in the throes of dismemberment. Lincoln himself, who had been elected by a popular vote a million smaller than that received by the three defeated candidates, was an object of distrust and prejudice to a majority of the people and of ridicule and contempt to a not inconsiderable minority. His party was made up of discordant elements; and the opposite party was suspicious and hostile. There were no leaders who commanded the confidence of the public, either in statesmanship or in war. The army, small as it was, was scattered, and many of its officers had deserted. There was no money in the treasury, and the national credit was sinking. The seceding states, which had long been preparing for the contest, immediately organized under a strong central government; and their organization, their unity of purpose and community of interest, their previous habits and experience, their matchless generals, and their immediately available military resources gave them at the outset an enormous advantage. The great powers of Western Europe manifested a cold neutrality, and cherished a secret hostility, towards the national government; and their sympathy and moral support were given to the confederates. Yet from all these dire circumstances the inexperienced man of the prairies wrested immortal victory. He united his own party, enlisted the support of the opposition, and won the confidence of the people. At his call soldiers poured into the army and money into the treasury. Terrible disasters were followed by brilliant victories, by Vicksburg, by Gettysburg, and by the march from Atlanta to the Sea. Almost by acclamation the great leader was re-elected to the Presidency. And before sealing the immortal work with his martyr's blood, he saw the confederacy overthrown, the union re-established, and the slave set free. His memory is the most precious heritage of the American people; they recognize in their great war President — "kindly-earnest, brave, foreseeing man "

— a fellow-worker with Divine Providence.

This is the man of action, engaged in noble struggles, whose testimony I would seek in regard to religious faith. If Darwin's spiritual powers were atrophied by his absorbing preoccupation with the phenomena of the natural world; if, like the domestic duck whose wings, he tells us, have become shrunken and useless from disuse, the pinions of his own soul, disabled for want of exercise, refused to soar above the solid ground of nature's familiar scenes and occurences; and if the glances he sometimes cast into the depths of the distant heavens only brought him a deeper sense of "the heavy and the weary weight of all this unintelligible world," which he nevertheless conjectured must have a Divine Artificer; — if, I say, the most scientific of theoretic inquirers has no experience that brings authentic tidings of a reality beyond the veil of sense, let us turn to the doer of deeds of justice and righteousness and see whether the orbit of his best endeavor has ever seen the light of Infinite Goodness or felt the touch and thrill of Will Omnipotent.

Now, it is a happy circumstance that our "first American," as Lowell calls him, leaves us in no doubt either as to the fact of his faith in God or as to the power which that faith gave him in doing what history, I think, will pronounce the supreme work of the nineteenth century. Indeed, Lincoln talked with such serene confidence, such perfect assurance of pious faith, that some persons believed him to be superstitious. Certainly the veil between the natural and the supranatural was for him neither thick nor opaque. God ruled the world in righteousness, and men were the servants and instruments of His rule: such was the faith that thrilled in every drop of Lincoln's blood. "I know," he said to his friend Bateman not long before the war, "I know that there is a God, and He hates injustice and slavery." And again: "Douglas don't care whether slavery is voted up or down, but God cares, and humanity cares, and I care; and with God's help I shall not fail." A greater than Lincoln has said: "If any man will do His will, he shall know of the doctrine, whether it be of God." Moral action is the road to spiritual intuition.

This great truth, which the world is always ignoring, was splendidly verified in and by Lincoln. He took his stand on principle; he did what was right; and the right approved itself in his consciousness the law and will of a righteous God, with infinite power at its disposal. Thus right makes might. Thus Lincoln saved the Republic. And I wish to say deliberately, after reading many lives of Lincoln and trying to understand the history of the Civil War, that in my opinion the Union could not have been restored without the unseen, but none the less real, power which came to the nation through Lincoln's belief in God and confidence in His moral government of the world.

Nor was Lincoln's faith a matter of tradition. It rested on no external authority whatever, not even the Bible, — a book which, with Shakespeare, always lay on his table and which he read every day. "No," he said in answer to Chittenden's question whether it must not all depend on our faith in the Bible, "no, there is the element of personal experience." And, let me add, that this basis of religion is precisely the same as that which science enjoys; for the principle of the uniformity of nature, on which all science rests, is simply a postulate or axiom which experience confirms but cannot demonstrate. Faith in God we cannot prove though it approves itself to us.

It is true that Lincoln never joined any of the churches. He had mental reservations about their long and complicated statements of Christian doctrine. But he said to Congressman Deming that, when any church would inscribe over its altar, as the sole qualification for membership, "the Saviour's condensed statement" of the substance of both law and gospel: "Thou shalt love the Lord thy God with all thy heart, and with all thy soul, and with all thy strength, and with all thy mind; and thy neighbor as thyself," that church would he join with all his heart and soul.

But this confession of faith brings me back to Huxley, whom I have too long kept in the background. Once and, so far as I know, once only, Huxley gives us his own positive conception of religion. It is in the essay on "Genesis *versus* Nature." He first quotes the verse from Micah:

"And what doth the Lord require of thee, but to do justly, and to love mercy, and to walk humbly with thy God"; and then he adds this statement: "If any so-called religion takes away from this great saying of Micah, I think it wantonly mutilates, while, if it adds thereto, I think it obscures the perfect ideal of religion."

If this was Huxley's own religion, — and that I take to be the meaning of the passage, — then, in spite of all his professional and controversial Agnosticism, Huxley's personal faith would seem to have been not so different from Lincoln's, although it was probably neither so sure nor so fervent. This blending of conservatism in essential faith, quietly and personally held, with radicalism provoked by disputation over unessential dogmas, is no unique phenomenon in human nature. Even Hume, when he was told that he had subverted the principles of religion, replied that he threw out his speculations to entertain the learned and metaphysical world, yet he did "not think so differently from the rest of the world" as people imagined. It may well be, therefore, that if we go deep enough we shall find that the difference in faith between Huxley, the Agnostic scientist, and Lincoln, the Christian statesman, is not a fundamental one. The one has voiced his creed in the golden text of the Old Testament, the other in the golden text of the New; but the substance of the confession is the same in both. If this faith be not the Christian religion, it was certainly the religion of Christ. Yet Huxley, living, was the last man in the world to force himself into an unwilling communion. And, now that he is gone, piety forbids us to rank him with those who might disown him. Let us leave him, therefore, in the pomerium of Agnosticism. But if any wise ruler in Israel, if any intelligent citizen of the *Civitas Dei*, will hold converse with him there and learn something of his heart and life as well as of his intellect, he will, I think, return to us and report in the spirit of that profound epigram in which Carlyle recorded his first meeting with John Sterling, that they did " very well " together, " arguing copiously, but *except* in opinion not disagreeing."

G

PART II

PHILOSOPHICAL AGNOSTICISM

" For now we see through a glass, darkly ;
. . . now I know in part."

PHILOSOPHICAL AGNOSTICISM

THE Agnostic is one who holds that he has no knowledge of God, or, indeed, that the human mind is incapable of reaching a knowledge of God. Though this creed is not new, it has reached its highest potency of expression in modern times, and the name by which it is designated is of very recent origin. The linguistic mintage we owe to Professor Huxley. Borrowing the word " Agnostic " from the Greek designation of that "unknown " God whose altar Paul saw at Athens, he invested the imported term with a metaphysical meaning to which the original was neutral and indifferent, and sent it forth to proclaim to the modern world a mental incompetency in regard to the knowing of God, which up to this time had been merely implied by the more general term of scepticism. The new name was coined in 1869. That an appellation was needed proves that the Agnostic sect was coming into prominence. The church it would supersede was an accomplished fact when at Antioch the disciples were first called Christians.

The canonical writings of the Agnostic sect all antedate the year of its christening. We have not space here to examine them or even to enumerate their titles. But whether the authors be rationalistic or empirical philosophers, Christian divines or positivist scientists, the burden of their message is always the incapacity of the human mind to know anything but the phenomena of the sensible world, or the contradictions in which it is involved when it essays to reach Infinite and Absolute Reality. This is the refrain, somewhat monotonous it must be admitted, of Mr. Herbert Spencer's metaphysics, varied only by denunciation of those whose religion consists in humble faith in God, not in confident assurance of His incognizableness. This is the universal incantation by which Dean Mansel would exorcise doubt of revealed religion, as though by poisoning the chalice of natural knowledge he could commend to our lips the divine

wine of revelation ! Both Mansel and Mr.
Spencer borrow the doctrine of nescience
from Hamilton, in whose system it appears
as the result of an inauspicious attempt to
combine the speculations of Kant with
the sober, home-staying philosophy of the
Scottish school. With Kant and Hume
(who provoked Kant into becoming a
critical philosopher) we reach the foun-
tain-heads of modern Agnosticism. Now
Kant and Hume also mark an epoch in
the history of philosophy, — for the reason, as generally stated, that they were
the first to make knowledge itself their
problem, instead of the objects of knowledge with which their predecessors had
been exclusively engaged. But this is
not a complete explanation of the special
significance of Kant and Hume. Not
only was knowledge itself their theme,
not only did they propose to discover by
analysis its nature, elements, and sources,
but their primary interest lay in determin-
ing its limits, — in settling for all time
what could be known and marking off
from it what must forever remain unknowable. And each working in his own way,
— Kant with the pretentious apparatus of

rationalism, Hume with the simple instruments of empiricism, — reached the same solution of the problem : to wit, the knowableness of whatever we apprehend by means of our senses, the unknowableness of any other reality. Both agree that the human mind is incapacitated by its very constitution for the apprehension of God. Thus it was not merely by recalling speculation from the objects of knowledge to the knowing process itself, but by concentrating attention upon the limits of knowledge, that Hume and Kant gave a new shape to philosophy and laid at the same time the foundations of modern Agnosticism. Hume's position, however, has so much resemblance to the scepticism that constantly attended, and ultimately supervened upon, the constructive systems of ancient philosophy that one might, without straining the comparison, fairly recognize his earliest forerunners in Protagoras and Pyrrho and Ænesidemus. These are the prophets of the old dispensation of Agnosticism, as Hume and Kant are the evangelists of the new, or Mr. Spencer its great apostle to the Gentiles.

This juxtaposition of names will serve

to bring out a truth which seems to be little understood, but which is of the utmost significance, if we are to see Agnosticism in its true perspective. It shows that belief in the incognizableness of God is no accidental or belated phase of human thought. Whether Agnosticism be an illusion or an insight of reason, it is not merely a casual or modern eclipse of faith. However named, it has from the very dawn of reflection haunted with its shadow the struggling light of " divine philosophy."

Now a factor so permanent must spring from constant conditions. If the doctrine of the unknowableness of God appears and reappears at every critical epoch in the evolution of philosophy, as it certainly does, it would seem to have some necessary connection with the progress of constructive thought itself. A careful scrutiny will show that Agnosticism is the logical consequence of certain habits of thought, of which the human mind can with difficulty divest itself. Like every creation of man, philosophy is characterized by imperfection. The themes of philosophy are Reality and Knowledge. But even the best system has fallen short of a perfect conception of the Supreme Being and an infallible theory of the origin and nature of Knowledge.   Nor is this surprising, for philosophers are but men, and they bring to their speculative work the views and prejudices of the human race.   Now, partly in consequence of his animal history, partly as a result of his nature, and partly by the necessities of existence, man, tested by ideal standards, is prone to lay undue stress upon the things of sense, so that he is ready to treat perceptions alone as truth and material objects as the sole reality.   From this immersion in sense and matter, it has been the divine mission of philosophy to redeem us.   But here, as elsewhere, the real proves refractory to the ideal ; and philosophy has not infrequently succumbed to the error she was sent to overcome.   She has too often reduced Knowledge to sensation, and pictured God after the analogy of material things or mechanical processes.   *Such* a knowledge cannot reveal God, for neither eye nor ear nor any other sense can perceive Him ; and *such* a representation of God as an object among other objects easily discloses absurdities and contradictions.

Agnosticism, therefore, is the corollary of every sensational theory of Knowledge and every mechanical conception of God.

But Agnosticism is also the refutation of the sensational and mechanical philosophy, or at any rate its *reductio ad absurdum*. The human spirit cannot on reflection believe either that there is no Divine Spirit or that the Divine Spirit does not reveal Himself in the consciousness of man. Agnosticism, therefore, is a challenge to philosophy to frame a rational theory of Knowledge and a spiritual notion of God. And as nothing interests man so deeply as the knowledge of God, we may claim that Agnosticism has been the most potent factor in the movement of the human spirit towards the true apprehension of its Divine original. The Agnostic himself may not always be conscious of the function which he discharges in the economy of thought, and he may even take malicious pleasure in the reflection that he is a stumbling-block and a stone of offence to the theologians. But nothing is more certain than that the Agnostic's demonstrations of nescience fail to produce conviction, and their most general and permanent effect is to prompt thought to a consideration, criticism, and correction of the premises from which such a paradoxical conclusion has been inferred. The effort to paralyze reason only provokes reason to brace herself for another flight. The theory of nescience is but the obverse of the fact of science. The Agnostic, in laying down the limits of Knowledge, is a champion of the might of mind. That he can make such a demonstration is the refutation of what he demonstrates. A false prophet testifying to the truth, he reminds one of the description which Mephistopheles gives of himself :

" Ein Theil von jener Kraft,
Die stäts das Böse will, und stäts das Gute schafft."

Let us look at the matter a little more closely. Agnosticism affirms that we cannot know God. Its thesis is bound up in the two notions, God and Knowledge. The contention is that these terms cannot be brought together. Now, if this dogma be tenable, the reason must be either in the nature of Knowledge, as somehow inadequate to the apprehension of God, or in the nature of God, as somehow transcending the reach of Knowledge. Both forms of proof have been used by the Agnostic. The argument, however, in either form is far from con-clusive. Let us examine each in turn, beginning with the supposed inability of Knowledge to reach to God.

I. Why should Knowledge be disqualified from reporting the Supreme Reality? In the long history of scepticism, one, and but one, plausible answer has been given to this question. It has been claimed that Knowledge consists of sensations, and that, as God cannot be felt or seen or heard or apprehended by any other sense, the human consciousness is inaccessible to intimations, not merely of His nature, but even of His existence. The argument may be stated in different ways by sceptics of the ancient and of the modern schools, but in substance it has changed little since it was first put forward by the Greek Sophists, who derived it from the metaphysics of Heracleitus. Of course God, as a suprasensible being, must be declared unknowable, if you set out with defining knowledge as a con-geries of sensations imprinted upon the mind by the objects of the sensible world. But, as Plato already demonstrated, this conception of Knowledge is palpably false. It labors under three radical defects, which, although inseparably connected with one another, it will be well for us to contemplate severally.

In the *first* place, this theory treats knowing as a kind of mechanical process. It places the material world on one side and mind as an " empty chamber " on the other; and it pictures knowing as the filling of the chamber, through the conduits of sense, with outpourings from the external reservoir of being. Or, to use another favorite metaphor, mind, according to this mechanical philosophy, is a waxen tablet, and Knowledge consists of the impressions made upon it by the things of sense. The bald statement of this theory is perhaps its best refutation. Yet, as it is rooted in that materialism which is implicit in the constitution of language itself, we need not wonder that popular thought has always been in bondage to it. So long as we must use in describing mental processes terms which were originally framed to signify physical processes,

so long shall we be exposed to the danger
of conceiving mind after the analogy of
matter. With all his sense, circumspec-
tion, and insight, the father of English
philosophy did not avoid this error, though
the third book of the "Essay of Human
Understanding" is an impressive warning
against it. And what in Locke was occa-
sional, and to a certain extent overbal-
anced by a contrary view, appears in the
latest scion of the English school as an
habitual and radical illusion; for though
we may accept Mr. Spencer's personal dis-
avowal of materialism, no reader can have
failed to observe that his philosophy of
mind is dominated by the theory of the
"waxen tablet" and the "empty chamber." To all such mechanical hypotheses
there is one effective answer. The simple
fact is that mind is not material or like
anything material. It is a spiritual activity, *sui generis*, of which we are immediately conscious in all its movements, but
which we can liken to nothing else whatever, for to it, as subject, the world and
all that therein is stand opposed as object.
And it is an equally certain fact that the
act of knowing, whatever else it may be,

is no migration of things into consciousness through the avenues of sensation.
When we see or hear objects, the retina
or the tympanum is, indeed, affected with
vibrations of ether or of air ; and these
disturbances are transmitted by appropriate nerves to the cerebral tracts which
modern physiology has learned to locate:
but they do not drop over this utmost
verge of the physical into the mental
world, to which, indeed, they are not one
whit nearer at the centre than they were
at the periphery of the nervous organism;
and as for a metamorphosis of them into
conscious ideas, this is a miracle in comparison with which the floating of iron or
the turning of water into wine is easily
credible, — a miracle, too, for which there
is no justification, as the consciousness
which it is thus intended to produce is
given to us as a primal and ultimate fact,
being that which is nearest to us, that of
which we are most assured, and that by
means of which we know everything else,
including the cerebral tremors from which
it is sought to educe it. " The mind is
its own place." In knowing it is not possessed by, but itself possesses, the objects

it apprehends. Knowledge is not the product of things ; it is the creation of the mind. Juster far than the "waxen tablet" account of Knowledge is Browning's description — that passage of "Paracelsus" in which poetry and philosophy coalesce in a climax of beauty and suggestiveness :

" Truth is within ourselves ; it takes no rise
  From outward things, whate'er you may believe.
  There is an inmost centre in us all,
  Where truth abides in fulness ; and around,
  Wall upon wall, the gross flesh hems it in,
  This perfect, clear perception — which is truth.
  A baffling and perverting carnal mesh
  Binds it, and makes all error : and to KNOW
  Rather consists in opening out a way
  Whence the imprisoned splendour may escape,
  Than in effecting entry for a light
  Supposed to be without."

In the *second* place, the theory of Knowledge on which Agnosticism is based, misses in its analysis of the elements of cognition the most important constituent. It sees in Knowledge nothing but sensations. Of course this doctrine is of a piece with the mechanical conception of mind. If the understanding be an "empty chamber," if the cognition of things be the filling of

H

it with impressions from without, this inflowing material of sensation must make up the entire content of Knowledge. But we have already rejected as false the mechanical account of mind. And this sensational theory of Knowledge is obnoxious to equally cogent objections. For when we look closely at the facts, we find that, even if the sensationalist's contention be admitted, only the smallest part of our Knowledge would be accounted for. It might perhaps explain the qualities we attribute to substances, — red, sweet, heavy, etc., — but what could it mean by substances, or by the relations between them which constitute the most important part, not only of ordinary experience, but also of science? These constituents of consciousness are a standing rebuke to the sensationalist. There are others of the same kind, among which the moral intuitions deserve a prominent place. Taken together, they prove that mind is rational as well as sentient. Nay, more, the sense-element of Knowledge is of less consequence than the thought-element. Sensations alone convey no information to us; they are dumb and blank. It is reason which, present at every point with sense, reads into the impressions of eye and ear and touch notions that give them meaning and make them significant reports of an objective world. A purely sensitive consciousness could know nothing; it could not even apprehend its sensations; for apprehension is impossible without categories of thought to discriminate and classify. If Knowledge were made up of sensations merely, it would cease to be Knowledge. Thus sensationalism, if logically carried out, not only leads to religious scepticism but to universal nescience. It is the lion's cave, from which there are no tracks outwards. It may seem strange that the Agnostic scientist should rest in a theory which is not more fatal to theology than to science; but this only shows in what a lack of rigorous thinking his religious creed was engendered and what immunity from criticism any fashionable cult enjoys. Be that as it may, an exhaustive analysis of cognition will disclose reason as its vital principle. And to a rational intelligence the existence of God is neither less nor more knowable than the existence of the Self or of the World. The truth that mind is rational as well as sentient, is fatal to the main support of Agnosticism, — the easy argument drawn from the dogma that Knowledge is of sensations only. And with the disappearance of sensationalism, which is fast yielding to a juster conception of what Knowledge really is, the Agnostic wiseacres who have terrified the faint-hearted amongst us by pretentiously delimiting and circumscribing human knowledge, will find themselves without a vocation. No other generation, it is safe to predict, will see *the farce of nescience playing at omniscience in setting the bounds of science.* Scepticism may, indeed, survive and manifest itself at every forward step in the intellectual development of individuals and communities ; for deeper doubt is the first effect of larger knowledge ; but with the demise of sensationalism, this psychological shadow, though it continue to be called Agnosticism, will never again take itself for the light of ultimate truth or pretend that it can pierce even to the dividing of the knowable from the unknowable universe.

It has now been shown, first, that the Agnostic misrepresents the subject of Knowledge, and, secondly, that he misreports the elements of Knowledge. The *third* criticism to be made upon him is that he misunderstands the meaning of Knowledge. Even if the mind were an empty chamber, and in knowing it were filled with sensational material, the import of Knowledge — that which it signifies — would be something other than this process of furnishing. Now the Agnostic fails to discern what it is whereof consciousness gives us information. He blunders in reading the communication, and he confounds the parties whom it concerns. Sensationalism has so perverted his vision that he no longer sees realities, but images or even after-images. He will have it that in knowing we are cognizant merely of mental states, whereas what we know is always some Reality, and it is only by subsequent reflection and analysis we discover that sensational or ideational states were in any way in-

volved in the cognition of that reality.
The Agnostic tells us we cannot know
God because states of consciousness testify
to nothing beyond themselves. But the
fact is that Knowledge is a report of
Reality ; and if this fact be incompatible
with the supposition of states of consciousness as constitutive of Knowledge, that
supposition had better be dismissed to
the arsenal of physical imagery from
which it has been derived. That intelligence should make us aware of existence,
and not merely of its own states, is no
more surprising than that anything should
be what it actually is. How it comes that
we are cognizant of Reality, is a question
neither more nor less difficult than this
other, which is really its equivalent,
namely, How comes it that we are intelligent beings? That we are intelligent beings, is at any rate a fact ; and it
is just the nature of intelligence to have
converse with existence. This is no theory about Knowledge, but simply a statement of what it is. And the statement
is so self-evident that it would never have
been questioned — indeed, it would not
have been necessary explicitly to make it .

— but for mechanical theories alike of the knower, of knowing, and of Knowledge. Now just as the knower is not a waxen tablet, but a self-conscious spirit; and as knowing is not the receiving of impressions from without, but creative activity at home; so Knowledge is not an aggregate of miscellaneous materials in a storehouse called mind, but it is the unfolding of a living intelligence which, while open to all the influences of earth and sky, remains identical with itself, and so transforms or transubstantiates what it takes up from the environment as to make each addition the expression of its own life, — a life which at every stage of this process of differentiation and integration attains not only to a fuller revelation but to a more perfect realization of its own inmost being.

In the long course of this development, the essential principles of intelligence — the vital stuff of which Knowledge is compact — have clearly delineated themselves, although they are not obscure even in the crude thought of primitive mankind. At first, however, they are rather presupposed than explicitly conceived or expressly described. But in the dawning, as in the full-orbed, intelligence there are present three ideas, which not only fix its circuit but constitute also its real essence. They are the consciousness of the world, the consciousness of self, and the consciousness of God. These three realities are the soul of Knowledge, at once its essential substance and its ultimate goal. Its substance, for Knowledge at every stage, from that of the savage to that of the scientist, is an effort to realize more clearly what we mean by nature, by man, and by God; and its goal, for the progressive movement of Knowledge always returns upon its starting-points, only with a more exhaustive consciousness of the subject and the object, and of God as the focal source of their opposition and their union. Of course it is not meant that these three elements of intelligence are all equally conspicuous at every stage of its evolution, whether in individuals or in communities. On the contrary, there is first that which is natural and afterwards that which is spiritual; first the consciousness of objects, and afterwards self-consciousness and the consciousness of God. Not, however, that any intelligence is merely percipient of the external world; the meaning is simply that at first the objective consciousness predominates over the other forms of consciousness which, nevertheless, are vaguely present even from the beginning. The mental eye looks outward upon nature before it looks inward upon itself or upward to the common source both of vision and the visible — of intelligence and the intelligible world. But though the idea of God is that element of intelligence which is latest to develop into clear consciousness, — and which must be latest, for it is the unity of the difference of the self and the not-self, which are, therefore, presupposed, — it has not less validity in itself, it gives no less trustworthy assurance of actuality, than the consciousness of the self or the consciousness of the not-self. This is a point which philosophy has perhaps not sufficiently emphasized. At any rate, it is a point which the Agnostic fails to appreciate. For if it is conceded that there is an objective world of which something is known, and a subjective spirit of whom something is known, it cannot be that we are ignorant of God or in doubt of His existence. Like the self and the world, God is given to us as the presupposition of intelligence ; and so long as this evidence accredits them it cannot discredit Him. It might of course be said that we know no realities at all — neither finite nor infinite ; but this view is repugnant to common sense, it rests on a false ideal of Knowledge, and in practice it is impossible to carry out. Knowledge cannot relax its hold on Reality, for Reality is the substance of its story. And the point here emphasized is that our knowledge of God is the same in kind as our knowledge of the external world or of ourselves.

If it should be urged that, in the history of scepticism, the divine existence has often been put in doubt, one might retort that the self and the world have fared no better at the hands of materialists and subjective idealists. These historical instances remind us of the danger of operating with one-sided abstractions and turning them against each other. In the face of such arbitrary partisanship for either the subject or the object, or for either the finite

or the infinite, the fact needs to be stated
that as intelligence is conversant with nature, and self, and God, so it knows them,
not in isolation from one another, but only
in their mutual relation and implication.
We are not conscious of ourselves in sep-
aration from the objective world : on the
contrary, the latter nourishes our subjective life of feeling and of cognition while,
in volition, we react against it.   Neither
do we know the object divorced from the
subject : it is we who perceive it; ours are
the sensations which give content to the
perception, ours the thoughts which con-
strue it into an object possessing definite
qualities of its own and having definite
relations to other objects in the expanse
of an all-embracing space and the sequence of an ever-during time.   And as
subject and object mutually imply each
other, so, if Knowledge is to be complete,
they presuppose a principle of unity as
ground of their connection and reconciliation of their opposition.   Only on rising
to this unity, only when we "see all things
in God," can we see things as they truly
are.   The consciousness of God is the logical *prius* of the consciousness of self and

of the world. But not, as already observed, the chronological; for, according to the profound observation of Aristotle, what in the nature of things is first, is in the order of development last. Just because God is the first principle of being and knowing, is He the last to be manifested and known. If this sound paradoxical, it may be asked whether all experience does not show that what is nearest to us is the last thing to be known; and whether, therefore, a principle which is one with the very existence of intelligence should not be the latest to come into distinct consciousness and to gain verification and demonstration. Yet, from the beginning, human thought has been haunted by the presence of God. And beneath all the crude pictures through which the fancy and imagination of all peoples have endeavored to represent Him, we may discern the never-failing conception of God as the ultimate unity, who, in some way or other, takes up into Himself the differences of the objective and the subjective world. But, as the consciousness of the self and the not-self thus perfects itself in the consciousness of God, so our consciousness of God, which is no otiose and transcendent abstraction, realizes itself in all our Knowledge of the world and of ourselves. It is not more certain that the finite implies the infinite than that the infinite moves. and has its being in the finite. In the strictest sense, therefore, nature and man are the revelation of God. These two volumes may be compared with the Old and the New Testament. In both cases it is the later revelation which is the clearer. Man, as the highest point to which evolution has attained, best expresses the meaning and drift of the process and most clearly reveals the nature of the spirit which underlies it. Still the God who reveals Himself in man, especially in the moral and spiritual life of man, also reveals Himself in nature. All our Knowledge, therefore, of the finite is at the same time a knowledge of the infinite. It would be passing strange, if the light wherewith science is flooding the world and human life served simply to disclose our ignorance of God, of whom the world and human life are the express revelation. This illumination is surely not intended to smite reason to the earth or to light her "the way to dusky death." And she will escape from the confusion into which Agnosticism would bring her by the recognition that the spirit that fills "all thinking things, all objects of all thought," is known to us through our observations of nature and the experience of human history, but most of all in the stirrings of our own spirit, which wise men of old declared to be in the image of God.

From all that has been said, it would seem to follow beyond peradventure that there is nothing in the nature of Knowledge to warrant the dogma of religious nescience. On the contrary, since Knowledge is of Reality, and since the Infinite Reality is known in the same way and with the same evidence of assurance as the finite realities of the subjective and objective consciousness (which also presuppose the Infinite Being as the ground of their union and reconciliation), it is clear that, unless in a mood of finical but absurd scepticism, we are prepared to discharge all knowledge as illusory, we cannot impeach our knowledge of God or refuse to accept it as trustworthy. Agnosticism, so far as it rests on the supposed limits of our cognitive faculties, is in reality an utterly baseless dogma.

II. But the Agnostic, as was remarked at the outset, has another argument. He finds in the very nature of God evidence of His incognizableness. This argument is not so different from the preceding as might at first appear. Both presuppose an impassable chasm between human intelligence and Divine Reality. But the argument which has been already so fully traversed, imputes the estoppel of communication to a fundamental incapacity of the human mind. The argument which is now to be considered, explains the breach by the essential inhospitableness, inaccessibility, or incommunicableness of God. The pith of the one argument is this, that Knowledge by its very nature must fall short of God. The pith of the other argument is this, that God by His very nature must transcend Knowledge. The eternal divorce of the Divine Being and human intelligence is the burden of both; only, in one case the ground is discovered in a Divine excess, and in the other in a human defect. But the noteworthy thing is that the incompatibility of this pair arises not from a fault in each separately or in either alone, but from a fault which is due merely to their conjunction ; for that excess of being would not be an excess but for this defect of knowing, and this defect of knowing would not be a defect but for that excess of being. Consequently, in reasoning from the transcendency of God, the Agnostic is using the same argument as when he reasoned from the limitation of Knowledge, only he is looking at the matter from a different point of view — from the point of view of that which is known (or rather *not* known) instead of that which knows. This being so, it will be possible to dispose of the second defence of Agnosticism in much less space than it has been necessary to give to the first.

There is one general observation, however, suggested by this argument for Agnosticism, which it will be well to make *in limine*. As everybody knows, the Agnostic commends himself to men by an air of meekness and humility. His disclaimer of a much valued knowledge which others claim to possess, sounds like the voice of lowly honesty and intellectual modesty in a noisy world of self-assertive sham and pretence ; and even when he assumes the prerogative of rebuke and denounces those who will not enter into the kingdom of religious nescience, this reputation for humility is apt to palliate, if it does not altogether condone, the asperity of his chiding, while it may even surround him with the halo of a great teacher of truth unpalatable to a generation of Scribes and Pharisees. Now when the Agnostic comes before us no longer either as a stern reproving prophet or as a good-natured, ironical fellow with a humor for negations, but in the guise simply of a metaphysician who is to give a reason for the faith that is in him, he cannot of course claim immunity from any legitimate criticism to which those expose themselves who enter into this dialectical arena. And surely no other dogmatist ever laid himself open to a juster charge of defying his own principles. Something has already been said of the astounding spectacle of Agnosticism simulating Gnosticism in order to fix the limits of human Knowledge. But what shall we say when it

I

goes on to set limits to the nature of God Himself? Yet this is precisely what is done whenever it is asserted that God is so constituted that He cannot reveal Himself to the thought of man. How is this divine impotency known to the Agnostic who knows nothing but the phenomena of our sensible experience? If God is absolutely inscrutable, how can you say He must be of such a nature that He cannot make a disclosure of Himself or communicate with His creatures? Surely, in this proclamation of the Divine dumbness, the Agnostic touches at once the climax of logical inconsistency and the height of intellectual presumption.

But what ground is there in reality for supposing that the Divine Being transcends the reach and compass of human intelligence? In the theory elaborated by Hamilton and Mansel and adopted by Mr. Herbert Spencer, this ontological argument for religious nescience, though buttressed by minor considerations, rests for its ultimate foundation upon two premises which it is not difficult to isolate from the superstructure and its adjacent supports. One of these premises asserts that God is Infinite and Absolute ; the other asserts that man knows nothing but the finite and the relative. The latter proposition we have already canvassed in another connection. It is derived from a false theory of Knowledge, and flies in the face of our actual experience. It has been shown already that the finite and the infinite are known together, and that it is as impossible to know one without the other as it is to apprehend an angle apart from the sides which contain it. This is the truth in the much misunderstood doctrine of the Relativity of Knowledge. But, not to repeat or expand what has already been said upon this subject, it must here be asserted once for all that intelligence is not, and by its very nature cannot be, restricted to the finite and the relative in any sense which excludes from its purview the Infinite and the Absolute. These provincial limitations are altogether artificial and arbitrary. And with their disappearance the sphere of Universal Being stands revealed as the proper counterpart for the boundless scope and embrace of Knowledge. And when this point is reached — and it must be reached by all thinkers who accept *any* knowledge of reality as trustworthy — no difficulty will be created by that other proposition which predicates " Infinite " and " Absolute " of God.   For the Infinite and Absolute is not that which excludes or negates the finite and the relative, it is that which takes them up into itself and in whose embrace they find their truest being ; as, on the other hand, it realizes itself through them and would be unknown without them.   This organic and evolutionary view at once of Being and of Thought is the true corrective of that ontological Agnosticism which derives itself from the conception of God as Infinite and Absolute.   If it is the nature of the Infinite and Absolute Being to reveal and realize Himself in the finite and relative, and if it is the nature of intelligence to apprehend these realities, not separately but together, how, from such a perfect ontological and psychological arrangement for the meeting of the Divine Being and the human mind, can it be inferred that they must remain eternally apart ?   Manifestly the thinkers who drew this conclusion did not so conceive either of God or of human intelligence. Restricting the latter to the finite phenomena of space and time, — unwarrantably, as we have already seen, — they set up over against these phenomena the image of a reality which was not only to transcend them, but which, as infinite, was to be merely the negative of the finite, and which as absolute was to stand out of all relation to it. Such a metaphysical idol we can never of course know, for it is cunningly devised after the pattern of what Knowledge is *not*. Precisely because we are intelligent beings must we be ignorant of this nonentity. If it were real, and therefore in relation to other reality, we should have no trouble in knowing it, — were it not that the Agnostic objects, forsooth, to knowing by means of our intelligence because it is a relating intelligence, as though seeing should be forbidden to the eyes and enjoined upon the hands or ears. To know, to think, to comprehend is to compare and discriminate — to set one thing against another and to note their differences and resemblances. It is in this way that intelligence has come into possession of the intelligible world — finite and infinite alike.   Identity and difference are the poles about which all knowledge revolves. Comparing is the essence of the cognitive function.   We know man in relation to nature and nature in relation to man, and we never know either truly till we know both in relation to God.   But the Agnostic sets up the invisible picture of a *Grand Être*, formless and colorless in itself, absolutely separated from man and from the world — blank within and void without, — its very existence indistinguishable from its non-existence, — and bowing down before this idolatrous creation, he pours out his soul in lamentations over the incognizableness of such a mysterious and awful nonentity !   The truth is that the Agnostic's abstraction of a deity is unknown only because it is unreal.   And his argument has no bearing upon our knowledge of God.   The Divine Being, whose vesture is nature and whose image man ; the Ever-active Creator, in whom we and all things live and move and have our being ; the Holy Spirit, who nourishes the world and communes with the children of men : this Living God is known precisely because He does come into relation with His creatures ; nor is He recognized by the intellect alone — the heart owns Him with pious and reverent affection, the will bows before His righteous law, and our whole soul, yearning as it does for the Father of Spirits, is quickened and refreshed by His presence. This symphony of response from all sides of our nature confirms reason's assurance that God is not concealed from mortal ken ; that though the infinite depths of His being are beyond our present vision, we yet see " through a glass darkly " and, while not omniscient, really " know in part." Partial as it is, it is this vision of the Divine which transfigures the life of man on earth.

Agnosticism is only a transitional and temporary phase of thought. The human mind can no more surrender its belief in God than its belief in a world or in a self. Contemporary Agnosticism, strange as it may sound, is in part due to the great advance which Knowledge has made during the last half century ; it is blindness from excess of light. The astonishing results of scientific investigation have given us new insight into the physical universe and the life of mankind; and though, in consequence of the immanency of the Infinite in the finite, every enlargement and rectification of our view of man and nature must also involve growth in our knowledge of God, the first effect of this advance has been merely a revolt against the partial and inadequate representations of God which popular thought has inherited from the ages that antedate the birth of modern science. But the Agnostic fever seems already to be burning out. And as reason cannot escape from its three fundamental ideas — nature, self, God — and the development of reason consists in enriching the content of each and adjusting them harmoniously to one another, it cannot be doubted — and the history of human thought confirms the expectation — that reason's next step will be to modify or reinterpret the idea of God so as to inform and harmonize it with the revelation which science has deciphered in the operations of nature and the life of humanity. Nay, has not reason already to some extent accomplished her task? Does not the light already shine for all who have eyes to see? The conception of God as spiritual and not mechanical; as immanent not external; as working by law not by caprice, and with steady infinite patience not by catastrophic outbursts; as adumbrated in nature and revealed in the moral and spiritual qualities of man, who is the goal of evolution and the epitome and abridgment of existence : is not this conception, in combination with the idea of the Divine Fatherhood (which is the essence of Christianity), taking possession of the best spirits in the modern world and dislodging the Agnosticism by which it was preceded and by which, in a sense, it was originated? Even the greatest of living Agnostics,—Mr. Herbert Spencer,—while still strenuously denying that we know anything about God, yet advances so far as to posit the existence of God as indispensable first principle both of knowing and of being.

But apart from the peculiar perplexity into which our age has been brought by the attempt to assimilate such an unparalleled mass of new knowledge, both of ourselves and of the world, Agnosticism now, as in the past, has been provoked by, and is a reaction from, the excessive dogmatism of metaphysical theology. Indeed, many half-educated persons call themselves Agnostics merely to indicate that they do not believe the thirty-nine articles or some other churchly creed. The shepherds of the flock, judged by the articles of faith, make such claims to omniscience that the silly sheep, in sheer recoil, delight to browse on nescience. The theologians have sown the wind of Gnosticism, and they are reaping the whirlwind of Agnosticism. The harvest will compel them — it is now compelling them — to reconsider what and how they sow. And the analysis already made by the late Dr. Hatch in his "Hibbert Lectures" awakens the hope that Christian theology, having at last become conscious of its origin and nature, will slough off what this learned writer designates its *damnosa hereditas:* its affectation of infallible metaphysics; its supposition that the Christian revelation, which is the setting forth of certain facts, authenticates and guarantees speculations which are built upon those facts. The speculative habit was foreign to primitive Christianity. It is the invincible residuum with which the Greek world, though vanquished, endowed the victorious Christian church. The tendency to uncontrolled speculation had been inwrought into the intellectual fibre of the time through the pervasive influence of Greek ideas; and Christianity could, of course, be received only through this medium of apprehension. The Sermon on the Mount proclaimed a new law of life; it assumed religious and ethical conceptions without attempting to justify or even to formulate them; it contained no articles of faith; it knew nothing of metaphysics or speculative theology. From this simple starting-point, as Dr. Hatch shows, the speculative habit which the Greeks had ingrained in the mind of the world engendered the abstract and dogmatic metaphysics of the Nicene Creed. To a unity of belief in the fundamental facts of Christianity, which was insisted upon from the first, succeeded the demand for a uniformity of speculations in regard to those facts. " The holding of approved opinions was elevated to a position at first co-ordinate with, and at last superior to, trust in God and the effort to live a holy life." This is the bequest of Greece to Christian thought which Dr. Hatch characterizes as the *damnosa hereditas*. " It has," he says, " given to later Christianity that part of it which is doomed to perish, and which yet, while it lives, holds the key of the prison-house of many souls."[1] It is that part also, we must add, which has been most prolific of Agnosticism. The claim of the church to possession of an infallible knowledge has involved it in warfare with natural science and with historical scholarship. And so far as Agnosticism represents not religious nescience, but freedom of thought and inquiry, it has deservedly triumphed at every point. The church is learning to leave to science and scholarship the things that are theirs. But it needs, if Agnosticism is to be completely disarmed,

[1] *The Hibbert Lectures*, 1888. The Influence of Greek Ideas upon the Christian Church. By the late Edwin Hatch, D.D., Reader in Ecclesiastical History in the University of Oxford. — The quotations are from Lecture V, on which other historical statements of this paragraph are also based.

to learn one other lesson: namely, that as the religious life is vastly more important than the intellectual apprehension of its nature or conditions, so no interest of religion demands that we shall define precisely or circumscribe with a fence of words the Infinite Personality that lies beneath our faith and worship. It is forgotten that we know only "in part." Furthermore, for religion, as for art and life, the Vague has as much worth and significance as the Definite. It is otherwise with science, whose organ is the intellect. But it is a mere prejudice of the intellect — a prejudice against which the feelings and imagination must always protest — that we should deem what is vague to be less real than what is definite. On the contrary, the Vague is, in actual experience, not seldom far more real. And those who, in ignorance of this truth, endeavor to compress it into fixed categories of thought, are always in danger of dissipating its essence. The theological habit of defining what is known only "in part" and setting up the definitions as standards of orthodoxy, is a serious danger to true religion. As such metaphysical dogmas multiply, Agnosticism must abound.

But though theological omniscience has been a most fruitful cause of religious nescience, it remains, lastly, to mention another influence which, though less obvious, has been no less potent. It may be described as the *Zeitgeist*, the spirit of the age, the whole form and pressure of the time. Ours is an era of material progress, of useful inventions, of great practical ambitions and achievements. We have annihilated space and time and made force and matter our docile servants. But the hand is subdued to what it works in; and these material operations and utilitarian ends have undoubtedly reacted upon our own spirits. They have imbued us with mechanical modes of thought and material standards of worth. They make it conceivable that man himself is only a machine — a somewhat finer machine than the products of his own skill! Now with this conception of personality and this estimate of human dignity, faith in man and faith in God cannot easily survive; and Agnosticism is then merely the outward record of a spiritual paralysis already accomplished.

And to this blight of practical materialism came, as ally, the Darwinian doctrine
of the descent of man. Whether cor-
rectly or not, Darwin's hypothesis was in-
terpreted as degrading man from little
less than angel to little more than ape.
That such an animal should be the image
and revelation of God, seemed incredible.
As Pascal has well said, it is dangerous to
let man see too clearly how he is on a level
with the animals without showing him his
greatness. The effect in the present case
was the rise of an evolutionary Agnosticism which strengthened the Agnosticism
of everyday life and interest. And both
were reinforced by the Agnosticism of
certain men of science who insisted on re-
serving the appellation of "knowledge"
for the mechanical processes of weighing,
counting, timing, and measuring. Altogether the general spirit of the age, both
on its practical and theoretical side, has
been strikingly favorable to the rise of
Agnosticism.

But the historical and psychological
causes which produce a dogma are not at
the same time a guarantee of its truth.
The premises of Agnosticism we have

already shown to be false. When the baselessness of this dogma, which is seemingly so modest yet really so presumptuous, comes to be generally recognized, we may expect to see it disappear. And unless all signs are misleading, the night is already far spent and the dawn is at hand. But, as we strain our eyes to catch the first glimpses of the blessed morn, let us remember that, but for its humiliation and chastening in the valley of the shadow of Agnosticism, the human mind would not in our generation have initiated the most important reform since the Reformation, — the substitution of the spiritual religion of Christ for the speculative religion of Christendom.

PART III

SPIRITUAL RELIGION: ITS EVO-LUTION AND ESSENCE

"But the hour cometh, and now is, when the true worshippers shall worship the Father in spirit and in truth."

SPIRITUAL RELIGION[1]

EVERY now and then we hear the requiem of religion chanted alike by the spirits who mock and by the pious souls who have "no language but a cry." I suppose we shall always have professional mourners. But it is greatly to be desired that their services should not be prematurely given. If there is anything in the world that is alive and active, it is just this religious spirit for whose demise certain mourners go about the streets. The body of religion changes, the spirit and the life abide forever. To the assertion that religion is defunct, I reply by pointing to the intense interest which men to-day everywhere feel in religion. It was recently stated by a Massachusetts judge — Burke observed truly that we Americans

[1] This address was first given before the Liberal Club of Buffalo, and afterwards before a similar club in Boston.

like to appeal to the law — that there is
nothing in the world perennially interest-
ing but religion. The ground of this
dictum is to be found in the constitution
of humanity; for the human soul which
the things of sense fail to satisfy can
attain its true home and its complete self-
realization only in conscious communion
with the Spirit behind the veil. What
better evidence of the vitality of religion
is needed than the fact that millions of
our people go every Sunday to church,
notwithstanding the crudeness of so many
ecclesiastical dogmas and the sonorous
inanities of so many pulpits? Men are
too strongly convinced of the reality and
significance of religion to be driven out of
the temple by a caricature of its heart-up-
lifting services and ordinances. Furthermore, I assert, as a matter of observation,
that there is no topic — not even politics,
and still less science — on which men are
so anxious to be instructed. Man feels
himself akin to the All-Father, and he
would fain know more of the conditions
of his sonship.

There are, no doubt, religious changes.
But change is a sign of life. What is

dead is rigid and fixed. What lives grows, develops, and realizes its essence through differentiation. In this respect the development of religion is analogous to that of philosophy, science, art, or any other element of civilization. Compare the science of to-day with the science of the age of savagery. The investigation of nature's laws merely for the sake of knowing them would have seemed to primitive man an insane pursuit. The goal of his endeavor was to fill an empty stomach and so maintain a precarious existence. If he used his mental faculties, if he observed and made inferences, it was to procure food, to escape perils, and to overcome rivals. For fallacious reasoning, for imperfect observation, the penalty was death. In that universal struggle for existence, only those properly adapted to the environment could survive. This is the reason why there is so much truth and wisdom in what we call the vulgar, or common-sense, view of things. It is the deposit of the experience of the race tested by its adequacy for life. But this common knowledge kept all the time expanding. In ministering to their physical

wants, men were unwittingly in the ser-
vice of the ideal.   They noticed their five
fingers, and invented arithmetic.   They
measured land, and originated geometry.
They used the lever, and discovered the
first principles of physics.   They watched
their flocks under the kindly eyes of night,
and, looking upward, they dreamed of the
secrets of the heavens.   Astronomy is *our*
most perfect science.   By it we regulate
our watches, take our bearings at sea and
on land, and predict solar and lunar
eclipses.   Think of the astronomer, if you
would realize vividly the growth of human
knowledge from its beginnings with our
rude progenitors, who could not count
their fingers!   The poor savage had no
chronometer but his stomach.   As a
matter of fact, he measured the lapse of
time by the recurrence of hunger.   The
word " meal " means originally " time."
And the reduplication " meal-time," which
is not merely a peculiarity of our language, shows that the sense of time in
primitive man was pregnantly stomachic.
Time! Time!! like the rising reverbera-
tion of a dinner-bell!   The measurement
of time amongst ourselves is *astronomical;*

amongst our earliest ancestors it was *gas-tronomical*. Would you see at a glance the evolution of human science? Then note its rise in an empty stomach and its progress, often slow and always toilsome, to the mastery of the laws of the celestial universe.

Man has evolved, the arts have evolved, science has evolved. Evolution means growth and progress; there is nothing but has evolved anywhere in this universe of God. It would be strange, indeed, were there no evolution of religion. I care not how one defines religion, whether one fills it with superstition or empties it of everything but emotion; whatever it is, it has come to be what it is, it has had a history, and it is now in process of development.

Look first at the development of religion in the individual mind. The mind of the child is wax, on which parents and nurses and teachers set their seal. Our earliest education consists in appropriating the ideas and beliefs of those about us. Children get many of them, more or less consciously, with language; and their mimetic instinct, joined with their curiosity, keeps them constantly adding to the first stock. How much there is for any one mind to learn from the mind of the race ! A lifetime would be insufficient for any one of us to acquire and assimilate the mental products which the previous generations have transmitted. The utility of such general information is also obvious enough. Yet I wish to point out that something else besides the absorption of pre-existing material is required to make a man. Unquestioning recipiency, however far you carry it, is only the infantile stage of education. Many persons, perhaps the majority, never go very much farther ; they believe what they are told, and consider themselves learned when they have been told a great deal. I know an encyclopædic professor of theology who said to a doubting student : "Sir, I never had a doubt in my life." That man's mind was like the mind of a little child, not in its guilelessness, which is a Christian virtue, but in its absolute dependence upon others' thought.

The great Teacher bade men live each his own individual life, heedless of the rules and traditions of Scribes and Pharisees. This is the second stage in the development of the soul. The first stage is that of acquiescence and absorption in custom, tradition, inherited beliefs, and sacrosanct formulæ. These are our first schoolmasters; and the discipline they give us is invaluable. The impression they make is so deep and lasting that many persons never pass to the higher stage of free and independent manhood. Yet there is probably in every mind a certain growth in this direction. In the best minds the tendency is so strong that it issues in what, considering its nature and its effects, we may designate a spiritual puberty. It is a coming of age of the master of the house, who has hitherto been kept in leading-strings. He is disposed to call everybody to account. He despises tradition, sneers at custom, doubts the certainties of the creeds, and finds that nothing is indubitable on earth or in heaven. The assimilating soul has become reactive; the unchained Titan flings himself against every restraining authority. This is the stage of doubt that follows in normal mental development — if this development is carried along naturally — upon the stage of credulity and acquiescence.

In some form, though not perhaps in this violent degree, every thoughtful youth must be conscious of such an experience. It is, certainly, no uncommon thing to see the credulity and submission of youth give way to doubt, denial, and fire-eyed defiance. But this is an abnormal condition of the soul; from the nature of the case, it cannot endure. It is, in fact, the hurricane which precedes the settled calm; it is the darkness of chaos ere the spirit says, "Let there be light." The third stage of mental development — happy is he who attains thereunto! — consists in the readjustment of the old material to the new, in the discovery of a higher standpoint, in the attainment of an ultimate view of things broad enough to embrace all the facts we know of man and nature and God, in such harmonious relations as will satisfy the demands of the scientific intellect and the yearnings of that human heart whereby we live.

Credulity, doubt, reasoned belief, or faith: these are the three phases of mental development, and, therefore, they are the three stages of the evolution of religion in the individual soul. The child lives by faith as by his mother's milk; the youth, conscious of strength, revolts against the powers that have held him in tutelage; the man regains peace by a larger knowledge and a riper experience, through which the youth's doubt is overcome and the child's faith essentially vindicated. Scepticism is, we may say, only a halting-place, not a goal; it is the growing-pains of the spirit.

Agnosticism is the apotheosis of scepticism. It is scepticism as a creed, as a system, as an ultimate resting-place. Those who proclaim it strangely misread the processes and the conditions of our spiritual life. They make the aimless gropings of the youthful intellect an ideal for the thinking of mature men. Only, instead of the awful earnestness of the inquiring youth, they often affect an indifference to the great problems which oppress him. As though we could be indifferent to the highest interests of the human spirit! So long as life lasts, so long must we strive to grasp the ultimate truth of things. To shut our eyes to problems is an ostrich policy. Man is called by an inner voice to strive, and strive, and strive, and not to yield. Agnosticism would eradicate this noble endeavor. Its only justification, so far as I can see, is that men never attain the absolute truth, but only make successive approximations to it. But this very fact indicates with reasonable clearness that God meant our life to be one of constant and progressive endeavor. Such was, in the last century, the faith of Lessing, and, in this, of Browning. Our religious thought is to be on the growth. The complaint that no system is final rests upon a misapprehension of the nature of thought; for thought realizes itself only in continuous progression. The evolution of religious belief is necessitated alike by the constitution of the mind and by the inexhaustible character of the divine object of religion. Agnosticism is a passing fever of juvenile free-thinking.

So much, then, of evolution from the point of view of the individual soul. But religion has also an objective side. It is a system of doctrine and worship embodied in the creeds and rituals of the churches. When we speak of the evolution of religion, it is of this body of dogmas we think first. After the sketch I have given of the development of religion in the individual mind, it will not be so difficult to trace the development of religion as an objective system and institution, that is, as an established doctrine and mode of worship. Hitherto we have regarded religion as a process in the mind of the single person; now we are to regard it as a product of the mind of humanity.

The first thing to be noted in the early history of religions is that dogma occupies a quite inconspicuous position. With the history of Christianity before our eyes, this statement seems paradoxical. But the fact is that Christianity differs from all earlier religions in its insistence on articles of faith. Yet this dogmatic spirit, as modern criticism shows, was a late development in the Christian church, and a foreign graft upon primitive Christianity. Not belief, but ritual, is the keynote of primitive religions. Their essence is a cult, not a creed. They prescribe modes in which God's anger may be averted or His favor enjoyed. It is true that all religion presupposes the existence of God. But I firmly believe that no rational being has ever permanently doubted, or will ever continuously doubt, the existence of God, though men have called Him by different names, which best seemed to them to express the infinitude of His nature.

Certainly for the primitive races of men, God was an ever-present, a never-questioned reality. They conceived of Him in the two ways which all later thinking has followed, either as a Great Human Spirit or as a Great Natural Power, though never exclusively one or the other. Under the latter aspect, God was terrible as the devastating storm or the rattling thunder; under the former, He was the mild and kindly Father of the tribe. According to their experience and environment, primitive men inclined to the one or to the other of these conceptions of the Godhead. The tribes that personified the powers of nature dwelt in fear and trembling, with a haunting sense of alienation from the terrible Ruler of the world, though with the conviction also that the

God might be rendered friendly. The tribes that practised ancestor-worship, making God their Father, enjoyed a sense of union and communion with the Divine Spirit, who deigned to join them at the common meal and sit with them round the common hearth. For either class of worshippers religion consisted in cult, and in cult only. There, religion meant the rites and ceremonies — many of them very absurd — by which the hostile nature-God was won over to friendship with man. Here, religion meant the pouring out of libations and the offering of food to the ancestor-God who guarded the homes of his children. In both cases religion consisted of practices, not of beliefs. There was room for *hetero-praxy*, or an error in ritual; but there was no room for *hetero-doxy*, or an error in belief. Hence among the Greeks, — who are the authors of art, science, literature, and philosophy, who, in fact, originated all occidental civilization with the single exception of religion, — the notion of " heresy" was absolutely unknown. There could be no heretic in the primitive world. Cult was the first stage in the evolution of religion.

The second stage is that of creed or dogma. This is a step in advance of cult or ritual; for it presupposes considerable development of the intellect. I have already said that cults *imply* the elements of a creed, — God's existence and man's power of influencing God; but this be-. lief is implicit, latent, unconscious, and overlaid by ritual. It becomes explicit and predominant with the growth of human experience and reflection. The creed may be the philosophy of a pre-existing ritual. If so, belief in the creed becomes as necessary as the performance of the ritual. But the creed may transcend national traditions ; it may offer a new theory of God's will concerning man or of man's relation to God. Thus the Hebrew prophets of the eighth and following centuries endeavored to teach the nation, which had given itself up to forms, that God sought justice, mercy, and truth, and could not away with their sacrifices and burnt offerings. The burden of the Gospels, again, is just the fatherliness of God and the revelation of His love to man.

But such simple, undeveloped creeds are not the most striking varieties of the species. For these we must have a body of doctrines, belief in which is necessary to salvation. The perfect dogmatist declares that we are saved by faith ; and by faith he means acceptance of a number of propositions formulated by some council or synod. The believer wins Heaven ; the doubter — let him be *anathema!* Among Mohammedans, the standards require acceptance of the Prophet as the messenger of God. It is not so easy to describe the creed of the Christian church. For, unlike the Mohammedan, the Christian nations have been characterized by progress, and progress means more vitality. That which lives changes and varies. The creed of Christendom is not fixed, but plastic ; it is not one, but many. Only death gives the rigidity and uniformity which those good souls desire who are always seeking the living among the dead. A living religion is like an organic species; it never *is* but is always *becoming ;* it is always passing into new varieties. What life there has been in Christianity to produce all the creeds of Christendom, — the creed of the Catholic, the creed of the Protestant, the creed of the Episcopalian,

L

the creed of the Presbyterian, the creed of
the Independent, the creed of the Quaker,
and the creeds of all the forgotten denominations whom the church outlawed for
heresy ! But one thing is common to all
these doctrinaires : they hold that dogma
is the essence of religion, and each claims
that his dogma is not merely truth but *the*
truth. Religion is right belief, or orthodoxy ; and orthodoxy is my " doxy," while
a " doxy " other than mine is heterodoxy.

The stage of creed is higher than the
stage of cult. We must also observe that
the lower is taken up in the higher, as an
instrument for its expression. Thus in
the historic church of Rome, while dogma
is the soul, ritual is the body of religion.
The rites and ceremonies which constitute
the religion of cult, as well as the beliefs
they imply, are absorbed, and not only -
absorbed but transcended, by the religion of creed. But not only does this
latter make dogma the primary and essential element of religion, it also multi-
plies indefinitely the articles of faith. I
cannot here analyze the creeds of the
churches. It will suffice to observe that,
howsoever they may differ in details of

doctrine, they all agree in furnishing a theory of the Divine existence and government, a theory of the origin and destination of man, and a theory of the creation, course, and final purpose of the world.

These are all vast, nay, they are infinite subjects ; and it is not surprising that the religious mind, in grappling with them, should have fallen short of the absolute truth. What else could have been expected ? Certainly the natural understanding is prone to error ; and, even if we suppose God to have made a supranatural communication to chosen spirits, we can only apprehend as much of that message as our finite intellects can compass. In other words, given a revelation, or given no revelation, our knowledge of the ultimate mystery of things is but partial, provisional, and true in a relative sense. *In the past the churches have all sinned through ignoring this consideration.* They have claimed to be in possession of the final and absolute truth about nearly everything. The Christian churches knew that the earth stands still, with heaven above and hell beneath. They knew that the world was created in six days, and so much of it each day. They knew exactly how the first man and the first woman came into existence. They knew how languages originated. They knew why men must toil and sweat, and why it is that boys kill snakes. Nor was it to these problems of nature alone that the religion of dogma furnished ready-made answers; these indeed were only episodes in its main theme. Its peculiar boast was that it furnished a revelation of the will of God and of God's doings in nature and in human history. In the books of the Old and New Testament it possessed the truth, final, complete, and absolute, about all things of any importance in the life of man and God. These infallible oracles came from God Himself, who inspired the authors. The church was as sure of the actual authors as we are of the writers of current literature. Moses wrote the Pentateuch; Solomon wrote Ecclesiastes; David wrote the Psalms; Job and Isaiah composed the works that bear their names.

The arrogance of this dogmatism is hastening the close of the second stage of religion. It is the pride of intellect that goes before confusion and discomfiture. Dogma has conjured up the avenger, doubt. Men now begin, where they are thoughtful and serious, to ask whether religion has not had its day, whether the future generations will not be godless, whether the universe, which seems to us divine, will not turn out to be an atheistic machine. France well reflects the *Zeitgeist;* the youthful philosopher of the new generation, the late M. Guyau, has left us a brilliant work on " The Irreligion of the Future." Be the future what it may, there are few of the dogmas once held dear that now strike us as axiomatic. Astronomy has set the earth spinning, dislocated heaven and hell, and whirled man from the centre of the spatial universe. Biology and geology have revolutionized our views of the origin of our race and of the cosmos. History and criticism have made the Bible a new book, or rather a new collection of books, written, for the most part, we know not by what authors or at what dates, and put together, as a Bible, we know not on what principle. All the old landmarks, Moses, Solomon, Job, are gone ; and a restless sea of criticism threatens to engulf

religion with the records it adored.   This
is the so-called "warfare" of science and
religion.   For him who has eyes to see,
the religion of dogma lies exhausted on
the field.

Shall we then despair?   Lift up thine
eyes towards the eastern sky and see what
light is breaking just beneath the horizon.
It is the star which the wise men of yore
beheld and followed.   That mildly glow-
ing radiance is the immortal genius of religion.   Once eclipsed by nebulous ritual
and dogma, it shines now, and will shine
upon future generations, in its own inef-
fable beauty and purity.   Itself the breath
of God, its kindly light will cheer and
gladden the hearts of all the children of
God.   Religion is life and spirit.   It has
long been buried beneath creeds and superstitions of men's device; it now bursts
its cerements, and comes forth a glorified
reality.   The decay of dogma is the resur-
rection of spiritual religion.

Religion is life with God; dogma is a
theory of that life.   The mistake of the
theologians has been in supposing that
there could be no religious life without
a correct theory of life.   As though there

could be no digestion without a knowledge of physiology, or no imagination without a knowledge of psychology! Dogma was intended to nourish and support religion; its kindness, alas, choked and suffocated her. The creeds were meant to be the defensive fortifications of religion; alas, that they should have turned their artillery against the citadel itself! But spirit cannot be captured by mechanism. Life outlives the theories that would tear out the heart of its secret.

"Grau, theuer Freund, ist alle Theorie,
Und grün des Lebens gold'ner Baum."

The third and final stage of religion, which is now dawning upon us, cannot be so easily described as its predecessors. The religion of cult and the religion of dogma are things of the past: and it is a striking fact that we never know things thoroughly till we have gone beyond them in our experience. There is a sort of antinomy between living and knowing. "Has been," not "is," is the badge of all our knowledge, especially in the realm of human life. The religion of to-day, therefore, will be better understood by future inquirers than by us who experience it. But it seems to me that it may be described, not inaccurately and not too vaguely, as the religion of spirit. Dogmatic religion is retreating; spiritual religion is advancing. Henceforth we shall call that man religious who, be his belief and knowledge what they may, is possessed of a sense of union and fellowship with God. In the coming ages of perfected Christianity, religion will be defined as a man's permanent attitude and frame of mind towards the All-Father.

But, while it is true that we cannot describe very adequately the religion of to-day because it is a part of our life, of one thing we may be assured, that it has not broken with the past and will not be alien to the future development of religion. In the historical world there is no solution of continuity. The religion of dogma took up the religion of cult. The Roman Catholic Church, which holds belief in certain doctrines essential to salvation, at the same time uses ritual for the expression of its creed and worship. So in the religion of to-day, though spirit rises superior to dogma and to cult, it does not repudiate its convictions or wage a puritanic war against symbols. Spiritual religion will part with none of the elements which have entered constitutively into the development of the religious consciousness. We must be very careful to define accurately the mutual relations of the three stages of religion. They differ, not in elements, but in emphasis. In the religion of cult, the emphasis fell on actions of a certain kind, that is, on ritual observances. The worshippers performed the rites under the influence of certain beliefs, indeed, and in a certain frame of mind; both of these, however, remained latent and unconscious. The religion of creed lays stress on belief in dogma as essential to salvation; but it rejoices in the use of symbols, and it assumes, though not very consciously or explicitly, that a sound faith and a correct ritual will issue in a pious, God-fearing life. Now in the final development of religion, it will be explicitly recognized that its primary and constitutive element is neither cult nor creed, but what I may call the soul's entire attitude towards the Invisible, — an attitude which, in its highest attainment, embraces the creature's sense of dependence upon the Creator, the child's loving and reverent trust in the Father, and the man's fellowship with the Divine Companion who alone can satisfy the boundless and immortal yearnings of the human spirit.

To prevent misapprehension, it may be noted in passing that spiritual religion is something very different from ethical or humanitarian culture.   The enthusiasm of humanity is, indeed, the certain outcome of deep fellowship with the Father of Spirits, as we may see in Paul and Luther and many a less distinguished preacher of the gospel.   It is a blessed characteristic of our own age that religion has come to express itself so nobly in practical well-doing.   But beneficence is not piety.   To make the love of man the essence of religion, is to misread the latter and to divest the former of its supreme spiritual dynamic.   If the religious man is a benediction to earth, it is because his soul is bathed in the dews of heaven.

We have now traced the growth of religion as a process in the individual consciousness and as a product of the objectifying reason of mankind.   We have

found that, as a process, religious life
passes from credulity to doubt and from
doubt to faith ; and that, as a product,
religion develops from cult to dogma and
from dogma to spirit. These two lines of
development are parallel. In the life of
the mind doubt is higher than credulity,
while faith carries us beyond both to those
indubitable intuitions which are the constitutive factors of intelligence. Simi-
larly, in the external sphere, doctrines are
higher than ceremonies, though from the
highest standpoint each gives us only the
letter which kills, while it is spirit alone
that makes alive. Finally, credulity and
doubt correspond to the religion of cult
and dogma, while open-eyed faith and
reasonable hope are the struggling soul's
response to the religion of spirit. Indeed,
spiritual religion, which we have described
as the late fruit of the tree of objective
institutions and creeds, cannot be distinguished from that highest phase of religious life which, in the mind of the
individual, supervenes upon credulity and
doubt. At this point objective and subjective religion are one and the same. To
the religion of spirit, therefore, — a relig-

ion which is in the soul and for the soul,
— we may conceive historical progress
and psychological development alike to be
tending. When, from the least to the
greatest, all shall in this way "know the
Lord," the millennium, in which all good
men believe at least as an ideal, will actually have come upon us.

Towards this goal the race is slowly but
steadily advancing. The religion of cult
has vanished from the civilized world.
Civilization is characterized by a subordi-
nation of the physical to the mental ; it
puts material things to spiritual uses.
The civilized man has *come to himself.*
He can no longer be satisfied with mere
external rites and ceremonies. They must
be informed by thoughts. The religion
of dogma becomes a necessity. It will
probably long remain a necessity even for
a considerable portion of Christendom.
It is the religion of elementary reflection,
— the religion which asks and answers
questions about the deep things of God
with equal readiness and assurance. Its
questions appall the critical, but its answers satisfy the multitude. Indeed,
dogmatic religion owes its security to the

fact that man yearns for definitive and exact information about his own origin and destiny. By a well-known psychological law, the yearning predisposes him to accept any theory, but especially one claiming authority and finality. The religion of dogma has, therefore, always appealed to a supranatural revelation. Behind this intrenchment it is impregnable, even in the gross form of Mormonism, so long as the masses of mankind are swayed more by personal hopes and fears than by insight and love of truth. But the spirit of inquiry cannot be permanently repressed ; and in recent times it has dared to investigate the nature and grounds of revelation. The answer of the Roman Catholic Church was the decree of Papal Infallibility. The effect of this decree was to reassert the identity of religion with belief in divinely revealed doctrine, and to furnish an infallible expounder and interpreter of this doctrine. It committed the larger portion of Christendom irrevocably to the religion of dogma, for which, indeed, it had always consistently stood in the past. The Roman Catholic Church, rich in the reassured inheritance of nineteen centuries,

confronts the rising spirit of liberal religion with a serenity and confidence disturbed only by contempt.

The summary procedure adopted by the
Roman Catholic Church was not available
for Protestantism.   The reformers had
appealed from ecclesiastical authority and
tradition to reason, and especially to the
Bible.   They failed to observe that these
new authorities could not withdraw themselves from investigation.   The "all-de-
stroying" Kant dissected the human mind,
and asserted the incapacity of reason to
know anything of itself, or to demonstrate,
even with the aid of other powers, the
existence of God or the immortality of
the soul.   The image of the Bible, which
Protestantism adored, fell to pieces in the
hands of critics who wrenched from it the
secret of its origin, structure, and diversified meaning and purpose.   We have, I
am very sure, a nobler Bible than we lost
and a diviner faculty than Kant denied.
But, in view of the revolutionary work of
critical science, scholarship and philosophy,
— a work demanded by the spirit of Protestantism, — it is no longer possible for
any Protestant sect to wave the banner of

final and infallible authority in matters of religion. Protestantism, in all its forms, originated in the assertion of creeds or polities ; but the spirit of Protestantism has always carried it beyond its starting-points. Its history is the record of a growing disinclination to that dogmatic apprehension of religion which it owes to the Church of Rome.

This tendency can be illustrated by a glance at the history of American Christianity.[1] At the beginning of the Revolution the whole number of religious organizations existing in the Colonies is estimated to have been about nineteen hundred and fifty, or one for every seventeen hundred souls. The creed of three fourths of these churches, Congregational, Baptist, Presbyterian, and other, was Calvinism; while of the remainder some three hundred churches professed the faith of the Church of England. Methodism had scarcely gained a footing in the country; and the Catholics had not more than twenty-six priests with twice as many

[1] The historical data which follow are taken from Diman's *Orations and Essays*, pp. 201–264. (The census is that of 1870.)

congregations. If anything seemed probable in the future, it was the ascendency of the Calvinistic creed.

Now what American history shows is the decay of this creed, and, with it, of all merely creedal religion. The Methodists, who had no existence here at the time of the Revolution, are to-day the largest religious body in the land. The growth of Methodism may be attributed in part to its effective organization and in part to the missionary zeal of its preachers; but there can be no doubt that its main source of success is to be found in its appeal to the feelings and in its disparagement of the intellect in which Calvinism lay intrenched. The Baptists, who are nominally Calvinists, are now, as they were at the beginning of the century, second in numerical rank; but their fundamental principle, — the Bible, the Bible only, — taken in connection with their polity, has enabled them silently to drop the old theology and unconsciously to adjust themselves to the new spiritual environment. The Congregationalists, who, at the beginning of the Revolution, were by far the strongest and most numerous of all religious bodies, are now one of the minor denominations in point of numbers. With them the process of adaptation was more difficult, for the body had a deeply ingrained and inherited theological habit. But, after producing Unitarianism and Transcendentalism, the sturdy mother also made her peace with the anti-dogmatic tendency of the age.

There remain of the larger denominations who made profession of the ancient creed only the Presbyterians. And they have more than held their own during the century. The steady growth of this religious body, which never, at least in form, abated one jot or tittle of its Confession, seems at first sight irreconcilable with the view we are advancing. But this growth is to be attributed, not to the distinctive creed, but to the wise, orderly, and admirably effective system of church government by which the Presbyterian body secured to itself a full share of the fruits of American Christianity. Indeed, the creed, so long held with the resolute tenacity characteristic of the Scottish race that brought it

M

to these shores, has at last come to be felt as a burden too heavy to be borne. It must soon undergo revision. The result bids fair to be, as it was in the like case with the Congregationalists, a "compromise document." But the right of a liberal party within the Presbyterian Church will be established, and the last residuum of Protestant dogmatism will be officially opened to the leavening influences of the religion of spirit.

It may be objected that, while these facts do indeed show the decadence of the old theology, they fail to prove the decay of dogmatic religion in general. The objector, however, overlooks the all-important point that the religious movement which we have been examining was not so much a reaction against Calvinism as a protest against the interpretation of Christianity as a system of dogmas. Only half its meaning can be read from the modifications which have been made in the creeds. For those creeds, which are survivals of dogmatism, resist, like the Matter of Plato's cosmology, the transforming breath of the creative spirit. It is the penalty of the new that it must always settle with the old ; and for this reason its true character is difficult to discern. But whoever will compare the best preaching of the present day with the sermons of the earlier part of the century will be aware of an entirely different atmosphere and attitude. Of doctrine there is nowadays scarce a word. Fuller, larger life is the ideal held before us. The potential communion of man with God being assumed, as it always has been in religion, the whole strain of the preacher's discourse is directed towards quickening that potency into activity, making man's sonship vital and spiritual. He finds the quintessence of the Gospel in the text : " I am come that ye might have life, and that ye might have it more abundantly."

Few persons, who have not the opportunity and the taste for verification, have any idea how sweeping has been the reaction against the religion of dogma. It has gone on gradually and, for the most part, silently, but with the force and efficacy of a process in nature. The revolution with which the modern world has been in travail is now accomplished.

Yet the sight of it is a surprise even to the actors themselves. The hand is subdued to what it works in, and many of the clergy find it hard to conceive that the creeds which formed so large a part of the material of their theological training are actually either obsolete or of minor consequence. But the laity, who have ceased to read them, are rallying to the support of practical and spiritual religion.

The goal of this religious movement is not uncertain. It is, as we have seen, not the religion of humanity, though humanitarianism is one of its manifestations. Neither is it simple ethical culture, though it leads to the full exploration and development of the moral nature of man. There can be no religion without God. And one great characteristic of the anti-dogmatic religion of the day is the conception of God, not as a capricious Power, not as an external Lawgiver and Judge, but as an Infinite Life and Spirit with whom the finite life and spirit that is ours may have fellowship and find everlasting joy. Personality in man moves out towards personality in God, and is met by it. The fuller our conception of personality, the truer and deeper will our religion be. It was a mistake of the older theologians, with their love of formulæ and finality, that they resolved the soul into a small number of definable faculties. It is one of the many boons we owe to recent psychology that it has taught us to recognize the Vague as well as the Definite in the life of the soul. Just in proportion as we see and reverence the mysterious depths of our own nature shall we rise in worship of the Eternal Spirit who is its source and ground. Spiritual religion is the conscious union of man and God. It defines itself only in the process of coming to be, and then only to the subjects of this process.

If the result we have now reached, along different but converging lines, be correct, certain conclusions follow as corollaries. These will serve to characterize a little more fully what we have ventured to call the religion of the future.

First, spiritual religion will maintain a social organization. The church is rooted in the nature of things. It is the essence of spirit to express itself, to manifest itself to others, and to form associations with them. Of all shallow speculations, few are more absurd than the assumption that churches are the device of priests and parsons, the mere organs of dogmas whose decline they cannot outlive. The fact is that every good yields its goodness only when shared with others. Even gross material things, like food and drink, lose half their flavor when taken in solitude. The common meal is the first product of civilization. Art and science embody themselves in corporate institutions which nourish and diffuse them. The church, too, is essential to spiritual life, in which no man can live unto himself.

If this was recognized when religion meant belief in dogma, how much more emphatically should it be recognized of spiritual religion! Creeds and rituals split mankind into sects; in spiritual religion men are drawn together by community of experience and aspiration. The religious man will feel (if he will but think of it) that he is an organ of a common life, which is the spirit of the church universal. Few things seem to me to be of more practical consequence for the future of religion in America than the duty of all good men to become identified with the visible church. Liberal thinkers, have, as a rule, underestimated the value of the church. Their standpoint is individualistic, "as though a man were author of himself and knew no other kin." "The old is for slaves," they declare. But it is also true that the old is for freedmen who know its true uses. It is the bane of the religion of dogma that it has driven many of the choicest religious souls out of the churches. In its purification of the temple, it has lost sight of the object of the temple. The church, as an institution, is an organism and embodiment such as the religion of spirit necessarily creates. Spiritual religion is not the enemy, it is the essence, of institutional religion.

Secondly, the religion of spirit does not need a unique or separate sect. Such a limitation would contradict the universality which, potentially at least, can even now be seen to characterize it. It is a Pentecostal outpouring which every one receives "in his own tongue, wherein he was born." It is a leaven working in all the sects. It uses what it finds to hand, recognizing frankly that the churches have gone beyond their starting-points, and to-day move toward goals which would have been inconceivable to their various founders. It pays little heed to the questions of speculation and church government out of which the denominations have arisen. It intrenches itself in the citadel, living on the best of terms with ritual and dogma which occupy the outworks. The maintenance of this non-sectarian attitude, which is a present note of spiritual religion, may be predicted for the future, as it can certainly be asserted of the past. It is a well-known fact, though the meaning of it has not been apprehended, that the decline of dogmatic religion in modern times has given a check to the multiplication of sects. The development of spiritual religion in America has had for its concomitant the consolidation of the great existing types of ecclesiastical organization. Creedal religion makes sects; spiritual religion uses them, and in using unites them.

Thirdly, spiritual religion will make its home with any of the religious bodies which recognize it. It will more and more become the condition and the criterion of church membership. As at the present day, so presumably in the future, there will be in all the churches men who, according to their various characters and stages of development, stand pre-eminently for ritual, for dogma, or for spirit. But the latter class is likely to increase with considerable rapidity. And it will shape the church of the future. The first business of such men must be to understand and sympathize with their brethren who have not yet escaped the bondage of rites and formulæ. One thing they must not do : they must not part company with them. How is the divinely ordained education of the human race to be achieved, if the children of light mass their torches and leave their less favored brethren in absolute darkness ? Humanity is a school of spiritual culture only (if I may appropriate a fine thought of Martineau's) when its members, who have a common nature but diversified attainments, group themselves into organizations of like and unlike, analogous to that of the family, which is the miniature typè of every moral organism. Consequently, if a true Christian discovers that the creed of his church is no longer tenable, his plain duty (other considerations apart) is not to leave the church, but to let his light so shine that others may come to a knowledge of the fact that the church is not the mere embodiment of a creed, but the plastic organization of a life which is spiritual. His insight into the real situation of affairs forbids desertion, even though he is aware that fidelity may be rewarded by banishment or persecution.

Such a course is apt to be denounced both by the religious and by the secular press. It is held that the defence is sophistical and disingenuous, and that those who plead it are undermining morality as well as religion. Now I will not deny, though I will not aver, that, in the case of those holding clerical positions of honor and emolument, the course here recommended may be unwise, for the simple reason that their motives may be misinterpreted by those who are always ready to catch the "appearance of evil." But, apart from this consideration of expediency, I see no reason why an honest man should withdraw from a communion in many of whose formularies he has ceased to believe. My reasons for this conclusion are, however, very different from those usually adduced. To read into the articles of faith propositions which they never contemplated, or were even expressly framed to deny, seems to me intellectual jugglery and moral paltering, of the most shameless sort. But this sophistry is the product of the religion of dogma ; it is the deposit left by the corrosion of doubt. Protestant Christianity, speaking generally, has put away, as we have seen, the religion of dogma, and is even now rising to the heights of spiritual religion. To this religion no one can be true who makes the creed the condition or test of fellowship. Varieties of church government have perhaps originated more sects than varieties of doctrine ; and in the near future it will be thought as absurd to leave a church because one disagrees with its detailed formulation of doctrine as it would seem to-day to leave it because one thinks its system of government not altogether perfect.

Doctrine, worship, and polity will, doubtless, in the future, be brought into closer
harmony with spiritual religion than we
see to-day. But the change will be
wrought silently and from within outwards. Agitations for the revision of
doctrines and modes of worship are not
desirable, if they concentrate attention
upon these subordinate elements of religion. If, as is frequently the case, they
help many persons to see that there is
something higher, they conduce to real
progress. Plainly, the religious bodies
best organized for development are those
which have adopted the principle of local
independency. Each church can differen-
tiate itself according to the requirements
of its inner life and its outer environment.
While the movement from dogmatic to
spiritual religion is in progress, these
various Independent denominations are
likely to be the favorite homes of liberal
Christianity. When, on the other hand,
the movement is completed (if it ever is),
the American preference for stable ecclesiastical order can scarcely fail to inure to
the benefit of the Presbyterian and Episcopal bodies. The latter has, indeed, some

advantages. For it has not, to the same extent, enveloped religion in dogma, and thus it cannot suffer so much from desquamation. The impressiveness of its liturgy and the grace and good sense of its forms — which in the seventeenth century filled Laud with a consuming sense of the "beauty of holiness," and in the nineteenth drew from Emerson the comment, "By taste are ye saved"— give scope and satisfaction to the æsthetic sentiments which in recent times have gained a very prominent place in the worship of all religious bodies. It is conceivable that some such organization as the Episcopal Church might ultimately become the catholic organ for that spiritual religion which seeks to express itself in symbols and in creeds. But the experience of a century suggests that in the four or five favored and consolidated types of "strenuously competing sects," we have a diversity founded upon ineradicable differences in the religious life of our people.

Fourthly, spiritual religion will lead to a modification, if not to an abandonment, of the conception of authority in religion. Authority is properly predicated of a sov-

ereign.   He has the right, or at any rate
the power, of enforcing his commands.
But if the ruler's will is law to his subjects, it is only on condition that it limit
itself to prescribing or prohibiting certain
kinds of actions.   Not even a despot can
command the thoughts and the spirit of a
man.   It is for conduct alone that the
sovereign is an authority.   Accordingly,
we conclude that in so far as religion is
conceived as consisting of acts or observances, — and these constitute the religion of cult, — it is proper to speak of an
authority in religion.   In the second place,
the term " authority " is metaphorically
predicated of specialists who have mas-
tered the facts and laws of any particular
field of investigation.   Edison is thus an
authority in applied electricity, Huxley in
physiology, and Zeller in Greek Philosophy.   These masters tell me what I should
believe in their specialties, and I accept
their teachings.   If, in the same way, I
recognize a man or a council or a book as
competent to lay down valid propositions
in theology, the man or the council or the
book is to me an authority.   Those who
identify religion with belief in dogma are

within the line of possibilities when they speak of authority in religion; that there *is* such an authority, however, is not a consequence of the inherent admissibility of the conception.

But if it is not impossible to think of an external authority — even a final and infallible one — for the religion of cult and the religion of creed, it is a contradiction in terms to suppose that there can be, ultimately at least, any authority for spiritual religion outside the soul which experiences it. Autonomy, not heteronomy, is the way of the spirit. But since we rise to spiritual life through successive stages of development (for the baby is only potentially a spirit), the agencies which stimulate and incite us to self-realization may, in a derivative sense, be designated the authorities for our religious culture. Without them we should not have reached the stature of perfect men, or acquired the freedom whereby the spirit becomes its own sole and absolute authority. This religious experience is paralleled by the moral. The source of moral obligation for the child and for the undeveloped adult is the will of the family, of society, of the state, and even of God. The virtuous man, on the other hand, knows that, while he is a fellow-worker with all the moral forces, human and divine, in the universe, duty would become mere legal or mechanical obligation could any one impose it upon the free spirit but itself. Yet if the good man is also a philosopher, he must recognize that that free spirit could never have come to itself, that the individual could never have developed into a personality, but for his training in and through society and under law, to both of which he has, nevertheless, in course of time, come to feel his own moral essence to be superior.

Just as law and society are authorities in morality, so the Bible and the church are authorities in religion. Through these disciplines we make our way — at least, some do — to the higher altitudes of free and self-supporting moral and religious life. But many fail to reach this stage; and even those who succeed would surely fall, if deprived of the guides and helps that led and aided their steps.

The function of the Bible and the church is, in this regard, educative. The noblest souls will feel most deeply their value, as they would be the last to belittle the function of law and society in the moralization of mankind. By its worship, even if it be merely formal, the church puts men in the mechanical attitude of piety; and, owing to the wonderful connection between our mind and our motor mechanism, the muscular exercise reacts upon consciousness and quickens the germs of religious life. No doubt Pascal carried the matter to an extreme, when he counselled men to take holy water and observe ceremonies, as if the rest would come of itself. But the general principle is sound: it is the foundation of the histrionic art; and one of our most eminent psychologists has come to the conclusion that joy and sorrow are the effects, not the causes, of laughing and of crying. But besides its ritual, the church has its articles of faith. The memorizing of these stands in much the same relation to spiritual religion as the learning of the multiplication table to the reasonings of the original mathematician. Lastly, no description could well exaggerate the value of the Bible as an agency for the development

N

of spiritual religion in the soul. This religion emerges, when the human and the Divine spirit meet and embrace. Now the Bible is a record, on a large scale, of man's reaching out after God and of God's communication of Himself to man. It reveals God as inflexible righteousness and as infinite love. What a glass it is through which to see the ever-living God! But how useless, when you put your eyes out!

A scholar, who is the ornament of a great church, was recently on trial for heresy because of his contention that the Bible, the church, and the soul (or what he calls "reason") are the three sources of authority in religion. His accusers assert there is only one ultimate authority. If the foregoing analysis be correct, neither party has the whole truth and each has a portion. There is only one ultimate authority in religion, — we mean spiritual and not dogmatic religion, — and this is the free spirit of man which finds itself in life with God. The Bible and the church, it is true, are, in a certain sense, authorities : they have the authority of pedagogues who train us up to the religion of spirit. The terms "authority," "finality," "infallibility," and the like, are, however, all borrowed from the religion of dogma. They are all inapplicable to the highest stage of religion, which is not an objective fact, but a subjéctive attitude — an ever-tending, never-ending process of communion with God.

Fifthly, and lastly, the religion of spirit will be not only theistic, but Christian. Christianity affirms that God and man exist for one another ; that human beings are children of the Divine Father who loves them with an exhaustless love, and that . they find their blessedness in a correspondent love of Him. This was the gospel of Jesus of Nazareth, and it is the foundation of all spiritual religion. But there is another sense in which, as I believe, the religion of the future will be Christian. Some liberal thinkers, indeed, have come to the conclusion that the personality of the author of Christianity is a matter of indifference to our religious life, if we are not deprived of his noble and exalted teachings. Others would be satisfied with a good example. But this position I hold to be erroneous. Like the religion of dogma, it springs from an inadequate conception of the soul as mere intellect feeding upon truth. But the soul is living spirit. It grows and realizes itself by contact with spirit. I am moved more by my vision of the personality of Jesus than I am by my thought of His doctrines. Spiritual growth is brought about by the impact of nobler souls on ours. Consequently, I cannot understand the Voltaire-like petulance with which, in his Divinity School Address, Emerson banished " the person of Jesus " from genuine religion. He thinks that you cannot be a man if you " must subordinate your nature to Christ's nature." It seems to me, however, that you realize your capacities only by coming into contact with their realization in others. The objectified self reveals the subjective aptitude ; and with the thrill of discovery begins the higher development. Spiritual growth is the attainment of those who constantly look up to higher personalities. Now if it is true of Jesus Christ (as Emerson says in the address) that " alone in all history, he estimated the greatness of man : one man was true to what is in you and me," then I should say that you and I are to find our own highest life by open-

ing our souls to the influence of this perfect and absolute personality. Nay, as
Jesus Christ was perfect man, so also, and
for that very reason, was He the revelation
and realization of the Divine Father. In
the new dispensation of spirit, as in the
old of dogma, He must, therefore, in some
sense, if not the orthodox sense, continue
to be our Mediator and Saviour.